The Goddess who jumped out of Hell

JAYA

I0132717

Become
Shakespeare
.com

First published in 2017 by

Becomeshakespeare.com
Wordit Content Design & Editing Services Pvt Ltd
Unit - 26, Building A-1, Nr Wadala RTO, Wadala (East),
Mumbai 400037, India
T:+91 8080226699

WORDIT ART FUND

This book has been funded by the Wordit Art Fund. Wordit Art Fund
helps deserving authors publish their work by providing monetary
support. To apply for funding, please visit us at
www.BecomeShakespeare.com

©

ISBN : 9789386487346

Disclaimers

This is a work of fiction. Names, characters, businesses, places, events and incidents are either the products of the author's imagination or used in a fictitious manner. Any resemblance to actual persons, living or dead, or actual events is purely coincidental.

This book is dedicated for my late mother, K.C.Ratnamma.

Acknowledgements

I sincerely wish to thank my late mother K.C. Ratnamma for giving me a sound Education academically which has made it possible for me to become a writer. She is no more with me to share my feelings but I have her blessings.

Next I thank my readers, especially the female community who have accepted reading my story as the noble hero is a woman who has shown the way for others when all the doors were closed in life.

My special thanks to my publishers, Wordit Content Design &Editing Services who have fulfilled my dream by a team of four or five to assist me in publishing this book.

Finally to the Supreme Lord without whose grace, it'd not be possible.

Jayan

Prologue

When this novel was written, I had no specific reason; it was merely a compilation of a list of stories recollected from my memory of past incidents in my life. All these stories were set in the late nineteenth century. A sad state it was then for Indian women and girls as they were cruelly discriminated by the dominating males whom the females could not question even if they were mercilessly treated. After marriage, they stood to face the wrath of the demon-like mothers-in-law and husbands on account of dowry and other issues which they brought forward after marriage ending in death of many sad women. This happens because they can't return to their parents but face the ill-treatment by the husband and mother-in-law. Moreover, girls were not allowed to go beyond their homes or pursue higher education. Naturally they had no other choice than to cling to their fate. It was not unusual to see that males used to beat, drag these poor victims out, in front of the public.

The fate of most Indian women and girls are still unchanged and the grim situation is nowhere different as they do not stand a chance for they fear to report these heinous crimes openly. On the other hand, I feel that if theyopenly defy and come forward to disclose the harm done, most of these shameless, unpardonable crimes could be minimized to a great extent.

I thought it fit to present in this novel, a noble woman, Smitha who bravely outfaced a number of obstacles in her way in spite of stiff opposition. She carved out her own path which led her to individual freedom and wealth for herself even though she had to leave her native country that was steeped in corruption.

She meets a series of adventures which were so thrilling and excitable and the readers may be astonished to read on. After having returned to India, she gets married and two sons are born to her.

In the first Part, the story is related in the first person and told by Smitha herself, but the second part, the story is given in the third person and focuses fully on her eldest son Bhasker, who rises to fame as a distinguished Cardiologist. More than that, it is made more attractive between him and Anna, his former school- friend and lover. The love bond is perfect and pure as to overcome all other love compared.

All in All, I am certain that the story told by Smitha and that which touches on the love and romance of Bhasker are narrated and told with perfection to excite the common readers. Teenage Readers from Britain and America have admitted that it is a great story told.

A great story that has been written in prose, conversational style and drama about a highly inspirational woman that brings to the readers an excitement totally different from others. Moreover, several incidents that follow one another portray a combination of the real happenings from the autobiographical touches of the author.

The story revolves around a central character, Smitha, who utterly disgusted with the chauvinism at her time, braves her way out, through her inspiration and opportunism. The second part tells the story of her son Bhasker, whose deep-felt love for Anna is so striking and admirable. The story focuses on the beautiful and wonderful as well as dark and painful moments in Life. Such is the truth about Life and the happenings are reflected in the Recollections of the past.

A book of Inspiration for all as there istruth & fantasy mixed admirably.

CONTENTS

CHAPTER 1 A GREAT EVENT

Great expectations were impelled with the approach of the great event. A mere glimpse was all that I had of his personage, as he sat chatting with my father a month ago, when the elders had unquestionably agreed to the match. The marriage proposal was for my elder sister. There had been bargains and demands from the coming in-laws, but my father acceded to their request, even though there was stiff opposition from me. The demands for money, house, gold, car, etc, that had been raised along with the proposal were not a matter of concern for her. The thought of marriage and a husband was all that hovered in her mind, and no matter how high the stakes that were raised for her proposal, she wanted father to give the green signal. Knowing her better than others, he gave in to their proposal and the day was fixed, allowing merely an interval of one month, to prepare for the great event. She wasn't even consulted regarding her opinion, whether she was willing to go forward with the proposal. The parents thought it was unnecessary, as they knew better what was good for her.

The love and affection showered on her by my parents were unparalleled, when compared with their attitude towards me. We were two daughters; she was the elder and I the younger. She was seven years older than me. But she was the apple of my parents' eyes and knowing their weakness for her, she kept pressing for one demand after

11

another, till a huge sum had been spent for her extravagance. The interest for fashion and jewellery was more than the aptitude she had for studies. Naturally this aversion to studies prompted my father to agree to the match, though he had to pay dearly. Besides, he had to support us, being the only earning member of the family and the expenses were beyond his reach. Nevertheless, he knew that as the father of two daughters, he had no choice but to get his eldest daughter married to the most eligible bachelor, who happened to come her way. Then there was his second daughter waiting. Such was the responsibility that he had to see through, if he has to spend the rest of his life in peace.

Father had to give away the wealth he accumulated over the years to his in-laws, demanded by them as dowry. Nevertheless, my father seeing my disapproval at him for having consented to their pointless demands, merely comforted me by saying that all that happens were for the best. But I was not satisfied. My whole being was transformed into a fury, focused on hating every male for asserting their self-elected superiority over every female.

"Who the hell do they think they are", I shouted at my mother in the Kitchen,

"You can expect more decency even in the slave market", I continued.

"We can't complain, my dear", replied mother "Society is like that. We can't change the customs; society had been accustomed to for years. It takes a noble person to speak out against these evils"

"Do you feel that no one has the courage to speak and act against its evils?" I enquired.

12

"Many have spoken and written against the cruelty of it," replied my mother," Besides, your sister is not as educated as you, and she has not seen the outside world. If at all she goes outside, she is accompanied by us. So she needs us and she is satisfied in marrying the person that we have picked for her"

"But, mother! Don't you feel that too many demands have been put forward in the bargain?" I said roughly, "It looks more or less like a slave market trading. If we agree to it now, how the hell do you know that they won't keep on asking"?

"But, my dear," My mother pleaded," We have no other choice but to give in; as your father has suggested this is the best choice that has come her way".

"O.K, Mother," I said, "If you feel that it should be so, but the evil is spreading fast like a forest fire for the sole reason, that parents having sons stand to gain without any effort."

"Quite right, my dear!" said my mother, "But we can't do anything when our society is on their side and such injustice is on the rise against those females, who have had no education, entirely dependent on those incoming hyenas, that spring upon the innocent panicking prey, whom they torture and finally consume them wholly. Not content with that, she has to face the torturous and dreadful demon of a mother-in-law, and the outcome could be a disastrous end, from a gas bursting into flames or being locked up as a lunatic in iron chains, supported by evidence to prove that it was a suicide."

"Poor thing!" I exclaimed and said, "What can she do when fate decides, that the devil and demons may harass her, till her courage is out of her. She, who has the courage to withstand the onslaught, may survive. But Alas!

The majority of the poor victims fall easy prey to the lecherous advances of the devilish mothers-in-law, who suck the resources of their victims dry, and not contend with it, hasten the end of the poor souls, supported by the sons, who with sadistic pleasure rejoice at the outcome of it."

"Mother!" said I, "How can we be sure that such an incident may not occur in your daughter's case too? The mental courage and physical ability to strike against the established customs prevailing in the society is lacking in her."

A sudden rage of fury burst in mother's face and the reddening of it confirmed it.

"How could you say such a thing, she resorted. "God forbid it. Such mishaps can never befall her. We have investigated and gathered facts from different sources of the incoming person, and the final verdict made only after the opinions raised by the elders on the issue had been discussed".

There was no point in having further discourse as she had a different view on the subject. I would never allow myself to be entangled by the clutches of the customs, as the horns in it would pierce and wound my inner feelings. A great awakening had occurred, with the continuing increase in the education of women in all walks of life. The liberation of women had started. Women having occupied important positions and status, even in political life, have proved beyond doubt that they could surpass the men, if given the chance. The clinging dependent women of old have been replaced by the modern educated women, on equal footing with the men, whose superiority have been erased with the advancement of the latter.

I felt as one, with the oncoming generation, liberating oneself free and majestic, like the eagle, soaring above the dark thunderstorm clouds, completely aware of the impending storm. Society is ever ready to criticize and condemn those who tread on a path, which invites criticism.

I was more than normal tall, being five feet eight in height and of a fair complexion. On many occasions, others had enquired the color of shampoo I used on my hair. Not satisfied with my replies, they asked the type of lipstick I used. To all these enquiries, I replied in the negative. But they were not satisfied with my replies. They believed I was not telling the truth. But I never applied any lipstick on my lips, for it was a natural red right from the time I was born. My Mom used to admire it as God's gift, for her lips as well as my sister's was slightly dark. They both used red lipstick to acquire the natural red.

I loved to be more realistic in my approach to life. I could hardly bring myself to follow the conventional system followed by all. I wanted a freedom that I believed was my own. I never could agree to lead a life that I felt was disagreeable to my way of thinking. I liked to move with the changes that I saw in the world outside. But society and my parents thought differently.

"Let them raise hell", I murmured to myself. "I choose to follow a path which suits me".

I walked the streets rejoicing in the company of both the sexes, unmindful of the glances of those with a sarcastic contempt in them. At college the teachers congratulated me for my practical modern approach to life. Students recognized me as a leader as I was never hesitant in coming to the forefront in times of dispute. I knew one thing for sure – when my time comes, I would never take the path which my sister has now chosen.

15

My sister was different as she had never gone far from my home. She had not gone farther than the high school that was close to our home. Her education was dropped after that and she had not been to the university as me. Naturally she had not seen the wonders of the outside world.

The day of the marriage was fast approaching sooner than we expected. A ripe season indeed as marriages were taking place within our community in the land of the supposed "God's own country", mainly within the state where marriages were celebrated with pomp and splendor exhausting the financial resources of parents of daughters who have to give away much to the would-be in-laws. I could see that a remarkable change had come over my elder sister. She could never bring herself to realize that it was actually happening to her. Everything was so sudden and unexpected that she felt that it may turn out to be a dream; she did not want to wake up but dissolve into that strange world she felt she would have the satisfaction that she desired. She had seen the person, and the recollection of the handsome features roused a peculiar sensation in her that she had not experienced before. In sleep and even when she was awake, the image of her would-be husband flashed in her mind. She was totally restless and tossing here and there even when she wanted to sleep, she could not get the sound sleep she needed. As a result, her eyes, pale and being drowsy, she appeared to be unsteady in her movements.

Even when mother started scolding her for her unnatural behavior, she simply uttered, "Oh! How handsome he looked. How lovely his eyes seemed to penetrate in me? Oh! I am blinded by my infatuation for him. Why are the days not flying past?

She was counting the days, hours and minutes as though it was moving at a snail's pace. The much yearned hour never seemed near at hand. Yet it was near.

Just two weeks before the actual event, I took my sister aside and asked, "Do you think they have made the right choice for you?"

My sister nodded and remarked, "I have nothing to say against their choice. Arranged marriage is the order of the day and our parents are wiser than us in this respect.

"If you feel that way", I said, "I am sorry to dissuade you from it."

"O Lord forbids it," I prayed. You, who are so gentle and innocent, can fortune stand aside from you."

The incessant noises arising from the activities involved in the preparations for the great event was enough to attract the attention of all and sundry in the neighborhood. My house was then invaded by a storm of activity and it did not cease even during the late hours at night. The endless swarming of the ants by thousands into the holes, working tirelessly, hoarding food for their use; like-wise the hurry and bustle in the house could be noticed by all in the neighborhood. The news had already flashed around and all were aware of the developments. Gossip travels fast if the agents are women but men too are not far behind. No sooner had the newcomers left than people flocked to hear the outcome of the visit.

"Has it been fixed? Who and what is the newcomer? How much did they propose? When is the engagement and marriage fixed? Did the girl like the boy?" These were followed by a hoard of other questions. My father had satisfied their inquisitiveness by explaining the events as briefly as possible.

The marriage season was a ripe moment for the owners of auditorium in the cities. Auditoriums mushroomed in several part of the city but they were not sufficient to cope with the endless demands and reservations from the public. Reservations have to be made several months ahead of the actual event. In the country- side they could conduct the ceremony in the religious centers. Besides, the availability of surplus land provides the opportunity for building large auditoriums housing unlimited number of tables and chairs and capable of accommodating a large number of people who are invited from both the bride / bridegroom's side. The expenditure for all these extravagances has to be met from the bride's side as the amount expended as gift money. Those who are affluent or whose income is far beyond their necessity could accumulate wealth over the years, thus overcoming the hurdles in life, overburdened as it is with the steep hike in the prices of essential items, soaring higher and higher beyond their reach.

My father having workers had constructed a large shed around the house under his supervision. When it was finished, one was awe-struck at the marvelous pomp and show it displayed. The sights of five hundred colorful chairs engaged in rows with balloons hanging down by the side from the roof transmuted one to a world of fantasy. This arrangement was merely to receive the invited guests.

The actual marriage was to be conducted in the auditorium, a few kilometers away for which two tourist buses and twenty cars were reserved in advance to provide transportation.

The day was fast approaching and a tingle of excitement could be noticed in my elder sister.

"Come, come dear! What beautiful cards!" she exclaimed to me on seeing them spread out before her.

My curiosity roused, I rushed to her. On seeing the attractiveness of the invitation cards laid out on the table, I was wonder-struck. At least a thousand were counted. Father had squandered a lot of money unnecessarily. People considered it as an insult if invited by post. On the contrary, they considered it an honor to be invited personally by my parents. Thus we were pre-occupied in inviting our honored guests numbering a thousand five hundred to attend the marriage ceremony. We had to make sure that we had not missed any one dear to us. A slight mistake may be seriously viewed as a grave error and will result in complete estrangement from the family matters by the object of our fallibility.

Jewellery in gold had cost more than the estimated cost but it could not be minimized as it could be viewed seriously by the in-laws. In most cases, the in-laws insisted on a sum and were adamant till its procurement.

I felt that my mind was not perfectly equipped to cope with present situation faced by my parents. The whole procedure and the superfluous demands brought forth by the bridegroom's parents was enough to persuade me to believe that the future would be bleak for my parents in the future. It would be better to be in hell than to be tossed here and there mercilessly by a society turning the father of sons into a parasite capable of devouring or destroying the support to which they cling for survival. 'Survival of the Fittest' is reversed to 'Survival of weakest' by a society which cares not for righteous but only wrong deeds. At last the moment had come, the moment that was turning point in my sister's life. Today the day dawned with promises for her; promises of a new world where the person who is entering into her life takes her to live happily ever after "as in" the fairy tales.

Absurd, isn't it, considering the fact that we are unaware of the person and the in-laws. It remains to be seen as to what fate stores for her. Being an arranged marriage, the disadvantages outweigh the advantages.

I would choose a partner to my taste. That could be inevitable if the person is not known to me and does not sympathize with me. You may call it love but the abstract feelings of sincerity and purity should be combined with love to attain the perfect love. Many misuse love as love for the attainment of sexual pleasure. That would be comparable to the beasts who craving for one of the basic need of nature desire the closeness of the male and female to the union of their sexual organs as in sexual intercourse.

Virginity in a woman or maiden has its place in an Indian Society. A would-be bachelor weds only a chaste woman, undefiled, untouched, unsealed by none but he for whom the virgin, ripe and inviting, awaits the inaugural breaking and penetration by his masculine power. A majority of Indian woman have preserved their chastity intact.

Naturally my sister was a little perturbed at the thought of the incoming first night with her husband. She knew that she was going to experience something new from what she had already known. Married life offers opportunity for a life- long partner, to have children and the joy and experience of bringing them up. Once married, she is fated to live with him for lifelong overlooking the fact that some may have the ill-fortune of being tied up forever to endure either a satisfied life or a life of wretchedness when the other turns out to be a rogue or even worse than that. But in spite of all misfortunes that may fall after, the belief that marriages are made in heaven make them to withstand all that follows in its wake.

As the day dawned for the great event that was likely to be a turning point in my sister's life; my humble abode was packed with people engaged in different activities. My attention was diverted for some moment to the beautification of the bride by a well- known beautician who had been summoned for the sole purpose of changing her countenance. One could only marvel at the speed with which her hair was tied in a fashionable style, her face washed with natural herbs, oil, soap, later dried and powdered with sweet scented powder, her lips polished with a scented lipstick till a sweet fragrance of the rose petals evolved from it. When completed, I was surprised at the transformation. My sister had changed into a beauty beyond comparison to the actual countenance I had known. It is remarkable that by artificial means, such changes could be possible. When she was led to a separate room, I could see that her hair was completely covered with sweet smelling Mullah Flowers.

The car in which she was to travel was decorated with scented costly flowers. On the front in bold letters arranged with these flowers was displayed "Parvathi weds Madhu".

The muhurtham or exact time of the marriage was fixed at 10.30am by the astrologer. The role of the astrologer is important in the sense that all arranged marriages are fixed only after jatagam of both the bride and bride groom are studied in detail and the approval of the astrologer for fixing the marriage date and time. The astrologer points out the date and month which is suited for conducting the marriage. Hindus generally believe that if such advice is not heeded, catastrophe is liable to occur in a married life. Even educated scholars and other affluent people believe the Astrologer and his words are given prime importance.

Relatives from far and near started arriving and soon the auditorium was completely occupied. Tea and cigarettes were served to the guests and most of them were engaged in conversation to pass the time.

At exactly 9 am the luxury coaches and the cars numbering twenty were speeding on their way to the site of the marriage auditorium. The reception took place exactly at 10.00 am when the in-laws arrived. My cousin garlanded the bridegroom in accordance with the Hindu rites. Then he was led to the auditorium which was immediately packed with not a vacant seat to be seen.

The musicians having started their marriage tune, the bridegroom ascended the stage followed by his father after he had received the blessings of his nearest and closest relatives, closely followed by the bride beautifully attired in an expensive pattu sari, the cost of which could be guessed at around twenty- five thousand rupees. It is a sheer waste of money for this particular sari is used only for this purpose. Later it is kept in the cupboard as a remembrance of this great day. Her hands were both covered to the elbows with gold bracelets and her neck adorned with gold chain. The Bridegroom was attired completely in white, white shirt and dhoti and his handsome features were most striking as he was extremely fair and masculine in his looks. Both of them, after standing before the people folding their hands in Namaste seated down on the dais ready for the marriage. The marriage ceremony lasted only fifteen minutes. Muhurtham and tying the taali on the necks of the bride was the most important part of the ceremony. Once the taali is tied, it is supposed that the bride and bridegroom are united as life partners by the Almighty lord and no powers on Earth could separate them except in a court of law and that too on reasonable grounds. The marriage ceremony over, the people hurried to the dining table for refreshment. Video cameras and photographers were busy flashing absorbing the whole scene on record.

The farewell or seeing- off the bride where the expression of grief by the father and mother for their beloved one on the eve of parting is most pitiable. We could not bear to think that she would be separated from us in a moment. Even my sister did not like the idea of shifting to live with her husband's parents. Tears overflowed from her eyes as she embraced my mother. It was a long moment that they clung to each other that my father had to separate them. Then she got inside the car that was decorated beautifully, beside her husband. As the sped off, she looked at me, waving to me that I started running beside the car, waving to her. The car increased speed and was soon out of sight in the flow of traffic on the busy road.

The sudden separation was unbearable for my parents at whose attitude I felt that some great loss had occurred within the family. Day by day, the intense pain they felt was comparable to the bereavement of one who was so close and near. The only alternative was to bring their daughter and son-in-law to live with them and the boy's parents were only too glad to be rid off the burden and the couple naturally enjoyed all the comforts in life at our expense. Madhu was gainfully employed in government service and he seemed extravagant by bringing gifts and other essential items to our home for each one of the family. My parents were lavish in their praises of him but I instinctively dissociated from his advances by refusing the gifts which were showered at me. I suspected the gifts to be a pretext to conceal his true motive for I despised his continuous penetrating gaze at me which seemed to increase as the days passed.

My poor father could only be a silent spectator as his son-in-law expended the bulk of the family income on parties and drinks. His aversion for my country – bred sister increased after a son and daughter were born to them, the difference in the ages being one year. The birth of the first child as a son is acclaimed as a great fortune by a father but Madhu chose to remain aloof for some time till all the expenses had been expended by my father. Feigning joy, he seemed to captivate the attention of all by his flattery.

One day after the delivery of his wife, he rushed in, saying, "You look so worn-out. Look what I have brought for you," uncovering a large bag containing fruits.
He sliced some into small pieces offering them to her.

"Why were you late?"

"Oh! My dear, I was held up by my boss in some intricate matter which was disentangled by my timely intervention."

Just then, he turned and looked at his baby lying by the side of the mother.
"He looks perfectly like his mother, fair and beautiful", he said turning and nodding at me.

Without a pause, he added, "I may leave on a business tour, for a few days", and he left hurriedly.
I turned to my sister and asked, "What has come over you both?"

"What do you mean?" demanded my sister.

24

"Don't take me for a fool. Something is amiss between both of you."

"He wants a modern - fashion minded woman," she replied, "I was treated as a clown devoid of sophistication at the parties and the poise of the ladies with their refined dignity and pretension of manners is really disgusting. A country bred innocent lady has no place in such a society."

"You could have withdrawn from such parties", I said

"By compulsion I was dragged into it. I abhor the ladies who with their pomp and show consume alcohol to get tipsy. They dance with other gentlemen after embracing them. The husbands too get drunk drinking and chatting the whole night. I refused to dance with his business counterparts and that aroused his anger. But being a fashion- minded gentleman he kept silent."

"Was he like that at home?"

"My goodness! You should see him then. He gets extremely violent, pulls my hair, calls me names and ill-treats me by inflicting bodily harm, cruelty as practiced by the low-class slum-dwelling drunkard husband."

"Does he always treat you so?"

"I am afraid he treats me like dirt. The very sight of me is disgusting to him and he seems to avoid my presence at the slightest pretext"

"Then why don't you leave him and stay with us for some time. Your absence may urge a desire in him."

"No dear, that would hasten his steps in the arms of the harlots and eventually his degradation. Besides I have to think of my children and the security offered in the relationship of a husband to a wife and a father to his children."

"My dear sister, you give in too much and so he realizes it. He knows that you would turn to him even if he goes astray." I said.

"But it's our fate and we, women have to bear it." My sister replied.

"Really! I pity you. Your submission in that way makes him to act, as if he could behave in whatever way he likes", I said.

"My dear! You are too young and you don't yet realize that life is different when you live with your husband." she said.

CHAPTER 2 BACK AT THE HOSTEL

Days and months passed and I was back at the college hostel for girls. The college campus was situated one hundred and twenty kilometers from the city in a vast area of thousand acres of land; the value of the land and the magnificent college building could well be over five thousand crores. One could only marvel at the ancient architecture as it was built during the mughal period. The monumental building had a lot of secret underground tunnels made for the ancient rulers to escape, whenever an emergency occurred. The classrooms for lectures were well ventilated to allow fresh air or breeze to flow in, and the construction was such that it was as though one could feel the sweet scent or fragrance of the forested area, which was situated around the vicinity of the college campus. Inside the campus, tall massive trees provided shade to the students to enjoy the companionship of each other. It was a common sight to see them romanticizing in the cool shade under the gigantic cluster of trees. The whole place seems to be a desolate area especially when the college closed for the vacation. At this time an utter gloominess pervaded the college campus, as very few persons chose to remain there.

The monumental building of the college was actually the palace of the ancient mughal rulers who ruled over ancient India. It could have been converted into a museum, as one would have marveled at the excellence of the craftsmanship

27

and grandeur of the building, which could have been utilized for that purpose.

There was a time when the luxurious and immense hall was crowded with the expensive suite of the sultan and his beautiful wives whom he had married from the surrounding kingdoms to add to his empire. The rich costly costumes they wore were the products spun by the best weavers of the nation. The wide hall was lined with the finest marbles brought from Rajasthan. The fortress was built around at a great height to ward off the enemies and though it was damaged at some places, it still remained to glorify the sultan's palace as it was before. It was common talk among those lodged in the boarding house within the campus, that the existence of an underground tunnel is a possible reality. But no one was able to find out whether it was the people's imagination, that had spread such rumors which turned out to be mere falsification of the truth, as such a tunnel in their opinions never existed. If it had, the owners of the building did not want the world to know the prized possession that had come in their hands.

It is not known how such a grand palace had come in the possession of private parties who had turned it for an educational institution, which had become incomparable with other institutions in the field. But the disgusting thing behind it was that it had become a place populated by the most elite among the wealthiest students, who had turned it to exhibit their darkest sinister actions for their sadistic ends. The building was so dilapidated and seemed to crumble down at many places; mysterious passages seemed to wind up and down narrow corridors and ancient sculptors of statutes that had a very ancient heritage were seen displayed at the dark rooms that were enclosed inside the building. Any newcomers who enter for the first time in these rooms would be startled to see uncanny figures here and there in the darkness that an eerie appearance seemed to pervade inside at night. I loved the gloominess and silence added to the loneliness that prevailed within its walls at the late hours in the night. At such moments I always had the feeling of goose bump within my inner-self at the realization that the presence of supernatural beings could not be ruled out totally from my mind. I have gone through many stories that have unnerved my senses into a state of uneasiness at the feeling that some hooded figures would attack me unawares in the darkness.

On my arrival in the college after the vacation there, I noticed an uprising among the senior girls gathering up for the greatest event of the year. Such things were a common occurrence as it was the time for fresh admissions and ragging the newcomers often turned out to be too cruel even to be mentioned.

The students who were lodged in the boarding were the daughters of wealthy parents who belonged to the topmost level of business tycoons and highly influential politicians who had no time to manage their children. These teenage girls had the privilege of enjoying all the comforts that money could make available but they wanted something else and sadism became their habit. They enjoyed it the more when they tortured the juniors.

A tall girl dressed in jeans from the waist to the ankles, her lanky legs tight in the jeans that her buttocks jutted out and she looked so tempting that a male onlooker would be lured to pat her bottom, as it would be too strong to resist. Besides her breast appears revealed in their splendor, the nipples seemed to push through the see-through blouse fitted at the back of her fair body with a zip that required only a push downward to reveal the magnificence of a well- shaped female body. She excelled in exhibiting her body by parts to attract the attention of male onlookers. She just wanted it that way.

"The Juniors! Shouted the tall girl in excitement". They have come. We should arrange a grand welcome for them at night, shan't we?"

"Sure, sure, Sheila" said the others in chorus.

"Remember everything we discussed before. This time we shall enjoy the more for the pleasure is ours."

"O.k. girls", said Sheila. "Neena, Lakshmi, Janet, Sophie, Asha and Molly may come with me. We can strike only when the matron is asleep for the wild cats stalk their prey only at night."

I knew what was in store for the juniors. Teasing, making fun and abuse in such a degrading manner had arisen in the hostel that the matron could do nothing to minimize the ragging undertaken by the elders to make the juniors submissive to their aggressiveness and heinous modesty.

Though the matron was aware of the development, she could do nothing, for the culprits belonged to the affluent and influential society. Having enjoyed the rich comforts that wealth offered, they were deliberately trying for new strange adventures. Most of the innocent girls were lured by hypocrites promising an adventure of high ecstasy and pleasure in narcotics. It is astonishing that while the narcotic sellers find no obstacles while they roam the streets searching until their prey is caught and hooked in their grasp. Once the victim is addicted to it, he or she will be at their mercy begging for more and more till final destruction swallows them whole.

Another sadistic pleasure- they indulge in teasing, abusing and ragging innocent girls younger to them. Ragging was tolerated in the beginning by the authorities as the girls resorted to only minor jokes and fun to become acquainted with the juniors or new comers. But now it has taken a drastic turn for the worst that students find sadistic pleasure inflicting physical and mental agony to their victims.

Sheila turning to her colleagues said, "Come on! Let us visit one of them." Suddenly seeing me, she said, "oh! So you too have come, come and join us in our fun"

I followed them and we entered the room where the two new comers have been provided accommodation. As we entered they got up to receive us. Sheila introduced herself and the others. Then she asked,
"What are your names"?

"Indu and Devika" they replied.

"Fine", we hope you will like it here.

"But unfortunately the Matron has given you a room which had not been occupied for months".
They listened intensively expecting her to continue.

"I don't want to reveal it." She said "But you should know the truth. Six months back, a student had committed suicide in this very room. It is said that this room had been haunted by her spirit and even the Matron fears entering the room at night".

Hearing this, their eyes widened in fear and the other girls nodded to confirm the veracity of Sheila's information. I, seeing the fear rising in the junior girls thought it best to

31

intervene but sensing my intention, Sheila warned me by a wink.

"OK Girls let us be off. A good day to you both. Forget what I have said. May be it is heresy but we felt that it was injustice that the matron had been unfair. We ought to speak a word or two to her about it. Oughtn't we, girls? ".

"Yes", said Asha, "Let's talk to the matron to set right the wrong done to these poor girls."

So saying, they left. But I lingered and said,
"Don't fear, girls. There is nothing to fear. What you have heard is not true but merely false fabricated lies".

But the seed of fear had been planted on them and the slightest disturbance could paralyze them completely in fear.

CHAPTER 3 STRANGE HAPPENINGS

I knew that something dreadful was to happen that night. The seniors always decided that way. They delighted in inflicting serious harm on the juniors and getting away from it. They knew that the warden would never dare to interrupt for they belonged to the higher strata of society. The juniors were in a way helpless if they could not face such situations.

I was awakened suddenly from a deep sleep on hearing a piercing shrill cry from outside. The impact of the scream was such that it could have been heard in the hostel by all. I rushed out in my night gown but no one was seen in the vicinity. None had the courage to investigate lest danger be involved in it. Sensing immediately that something was wrong with Devika or Indu. I hurriedly paced into their room. On entering I saw they were both huddled embracing each other, horror-stricken at something they have seen. "What is it, dear", I enquired.

But no sound was uttered from their lips. It was as if they have had a nightmare. But how could both be in this state? I thought.

"Come on! Tell me what has happened"

"The – the- the ghost . . . it was – was there, uttered both of them in a feeble sound.

"What ghost? Have you gone mad"? I asked.

33

"No, no … it is true, the spirit or ghost was here- all in white –ghostly and pale … it disappeared when we screamed."

"Were you both asleep?"

"No, No, we … we could not sleep… thinking about the suicide of the girl before."

"Oh! I see … maybe it was a hallucination."

"No, No … it was truly a ghost and real … it came quite near to us. Then it was gone…"

"Please", cried Devika. 'Stay with us for the night. We can't endure this anymore".
"OK", I nodded and said, "I will be with you for the night. Don't you worry anymore?"

I looked at the clock. It was twenty minutes past midnight. I switched off the lights and slept by their side.
I was awakened suddenly by the weight of Devika and Indu as they collapsed over me in fright. Holding them tightly to my chest, I saw a faint white apparition advancing towards us in the dark. I have read a great deal of ghosts and spirits but never believed the written stories invented by man to create meaningless fear, Bram Stoker's – Dracula, a frightful sensation to the world. Similarly, many have written of vampires and black witchcraft practiced by those influenced by the Devil. Man's imagination is unfathomable and many devil like characters are invented to create a shock – thriller.
Now was the time to confirm my suspicion about ghosts. Getting up with a surge, I advanced at the ghost apparition. Stupefied at such courage, the apparition took several steps backwards and retreated into the darkness. The speed with

which it vanished was greater than the speed at which I advanced towards it. I followed it and had a glimpse of it as it entered one of the rooms. I remained at the door; I heard faint voices inside.

"Asha, did you frighten the hell out of them" enquired a voice.

"That damn senior girl was with them."

"Whom did you mean?"

I recognized the voice to be of Sheila. So they were in the plot. Now they have gone too far. Their ragging was sadistic and cruel, causing mental agony and torture.
Sheila was furious and shouted.

"We must teach that bitch a lesson." Hearing this, I wanted to rush in and hit the devil on the head. But my better senses prevailed. They were many and I had no chance to fight them alone.

I returned to Indu and Asha and closed the door.
"That was no ghost. A senior girl had done it; you ought to give a written complaint to the Matron." They agreed to do so.

At the approach of dawn, it was a magnificent sight to gaze at the full red ball of the Sun in all its glory. Slowly, the red changed to dazzling white rays flashing in all directions as the sun moved higher and higher from the east. For a moment I forgot the incidents of the night but it was only for a fleeting second.

Accompanied by Indu and Devika, we related the incidents

to the Matron who promised to take action against the culprits responsible for it. On the way to our rooms we were confronted by Sheila and her gang.

"So you are trying to be a hero, Sheila said pointing at me. It would be wise not to interfere in other people's business."

"I don't poke my nose unnecessarily. But having done so, I have to see it through." I replied.

"Then watch out! You meddling fool!" shouted Sheila and swung her fist at my face before I could side step from it. I reeled backwards as the blow hit my shoulder. As I tried to get up, she tried to kick me with her high - heeled shoes. But, with lightning speed I raised my hand and catching her foot, heaved her off her balance and she landed flat on her back with a thud. Crying with pain, she shouted,

"Get her, fools! Don't just stand there!"
"Don't you dare",
I warned as they stepped forward. They stopped in their tracks as they realized that I could create trouble for my popularity among the students was well known. Slowly I got up and left them staring at me.

The next day I had hardly risen out of the bed when there was a loud knock at my door. On opening it hurriedly, I saw that it was Indu excited by the new developments of the previous night.

"What is it, now, Indu? Is it something serious?" I asked seeing the pale sleepless tired eyes in her.

"They came again yesterday and tortured us. Poor Devika had vomited the whole night. We are planning to leave the college hostel today itself."

I followed her to her room and Devika was lying on the bed looking desperate and ill. I confronted them and they were glad of my companionship.

Sheila and six others have resorted to unpardonable attempts at ragging. Indu and Devika were ordered to undress and when they hesitated, her accomplices forcibly completed the ordeal. Fully naked, Devika was taken to the bathroom.

Sheila said "Lie down and lick the toilet".

Devika could hardly believe what she heard. She was too stunned that such brutal inhuman behavior could arise in a female. Kicking her in the buttocks they forced her to lie down flat on the toilet. Asha dragged Indu and asked her to piss in a large cup. She was kicked several times until she urinated. The cup was handed over to Sheila. Sheila poured the contents over Devika's face. Both the victims were relieved when these crazy she – devils left, feeling that enough ragging has been done for the day.

When the matron came, I pointed out and said,
"Such cruelty! Such inhuman acts! They should be punished."

"I have reported to their parents. But they don't care," said the matron.

"Report to the police, then. They should be put behind bars." I retaliated.
"No use, my dear, parents would easily get bail or release for them and they would be in the scene with greater revenge."

"In that case the victims have to vacate the place. It seems that the Principal and you are helpless to prevent such heinous atrocious deeds for fear of losing the purse offered by these affluent classes or maybe you think so, don't you? It does not concern you".

So saying, I left her staring blankly at me.

The next day while I was having breakfast, I heard a commotion outside. After hurriedly devouring the meager quota allotted for me, I rushed outside anxious to know the cause. Immediately I noticed the matron in a panic stricken state, her face convulsed in deep shock alarmed at something which had affected her. I comforted her by putting my arms and shoulders around her.

"Madam, I enquired, what has happened?" "They - - they are missing" – uttered the Matron in fear.

"Who are missing", I asked anxious to learn more.

"Devika and Indu", said the matron.

"They have run away—alas! What am I doing? What can I say to their parents? As a Matron I am done for. The management will sack me - - oh - - oh - - I can't face it".

"Stop your wailing, Madam," I pleaded. "Let us find out if someone has seen them. Perhaps the watch man may have - - - - he was on duty."

It was at this juncture that one of the girls who were a party at the ragging the previous night hurried towards us.

"Matron- - Madam - - I saw the girls - - - - they were dragged from the road into a van by some young men - - - the van then sped away with them."
I caught her in a wild grip hurting her.

"Tell us the truth - - you devil." I shouted at her.

"It is the truth. The men took them by force. I was too frightened to intervene, so I hid in a bush. I saw the evil men take the girls who were fighting for their lives.
 "Did you note down the number?"

"Sure! It was a blue Maruti Van ... KL-01-C 45658" She said.

"Come on! Let us inform the Police",

I almost pushed the matron at my effort to take the receiver in my hand but the Matron was quicker. She got the Superintendent of Police on the line and she sought his assistance immediately.

Within no time a Police Jeep arrived at the hostel. The S.P himself stood before us, stern and authoritative, while the incidents were narrated to him by the sole witness but she was clever enough not to unravel the exact turn which had prompted the girls to escape the hostel only to be clutched in the evil arms of the scoundrels who were always on the lookout for easy prey to quench their thirst for sexual pleasure or for other money-making business racket they were involved. The S.P then demanded of the matron whether the watchman had been questioned.

"No, Sir, we called you, Sir, first ... stammered the Matron. He immediately signaled one of his men to bring the watchman.

As the watchman was brought before him the S.P advanced towards him and casually asked, "When did the girls leave the hostel and with whose permission?"

The watchman utterly oblivious of the happenings in the hostel uttered out "Sir, I don't know ... sir,"

. "What!" shouted the S.P. "Are you a fool?"

"Sir, stammered the watchman." I might have dozed off. ... I remember and saw nothing... I never saw any girls leave the hostel .... Sir ..."

"You fool!" said the S.P angrily. "You should be sacked. Three girls have gone out and you noticed nothing."
Turning to the matron, he said, "You should dismiss him. Such negligence of duty cannot be excused. But it is your pot."

"Well ... continued the S.P." I will inform you as soon as we book in the culprits."

After the sounds of his retreating footsteps faded in the distance, the rushing sound of the speeding Jeep was audible. Two hours later, the phone in the matron's office started ringing wildly. The continuous ringing indicated the absence of the Matron in the office. I rushed in and held up the receiver.

"Hello! This is matron's office." "Listen," Sounded the authoritative voice of the S.P,
"We have rounded up the culprits. The girls are both safe. You can come to the station to take them home".

"Yes, Sir, we are on the way and Thank you, Sir" I replied.

Putting the receiver back, I rushed to call the matron. She was seen talking with the senior girls.

I dramatically shouted," Madam, the girls are safe. The S.P has phoned. We are to rush there at once".

"Come on, girls", said the matron. "What are we waiting for, then".
Soon we were on a mini-bus speeding to the station. We reached there in record time. Devika and Indu were overwhelmingly glad to see us. The matron held them to her, turning to the S.P, she said,
 "Sir, you have done a great service in saving these girls from the scoundrels' clutches.
 "Thank god! Timely intervention has saved the day

CHAPTER 4 UNEXPECTED TRAGEDY

Two months passed without many happenings worth mentioning in the hostel. I was sitting alone, ruminating over the past events when suddenly the unexpected occurred like a bolt from the blue.

My friend, Sheila rushed in and in a hysterical voice stammered out,

"Your father is dead".

The effect of the outburst sent shock waves inside my mind and when I realized what she meant, I reeled under the shock and collapsed.

When I regained consciousness, I found water splashed over me with my friends anxious and full of sympathy.

"Take it easy", they said, "Your father is all right. He is taken seriously ill. Your uncle has come to fetch you home".

Suddenly my uncle came towards me. He took me up by his shoulders and supporting me with his arms round me, took me to a car parked nearby.

"I have come to take you home".

"Why", I enquired. "Is my father really serious"?

"I am afraid so", he said. "He has asked to see you, my dear".

I felt faint when the car started speeding to my home- town. A long journey lay before us. My mind was uneasy and in turmoil expecting the worst.

"Why should my uncle come for me in a car? The distance is too expensive for taxi-fare. What is the need for haste and the masking of the black truth from me? "The mystery regarding truth would be unrevealed – as black as ever".

I let my mind divert its attention for a moment from this masked reality to the sublimity beauty of Nature. As we sped in the car, I was fascinated by the beauty of the landscape. The mountainous road winding up and down in dangerous curves, the sight of the valley thousands feet below with occasional burst of the waterfalls rushing down at great speed scattering far and wide the foams and spray of water down below, reminded me of the wonder of Nature's creation. There were a lot of thoughts racing through my mind at this time. As we neared a narrow curve, the car slowed down. The sight which I saw excited my inner feelings.

"Stop"! I requested the driver.

He hesitated and when I insisted, he stopped. I stepped out to look down the Grand Canyon below. The valley was a mere spot far down   below with green meadows and the beautiful landscape inviting me. It appeared as if the arms of nature were calling me down below. Many have been said to have committed suicide from this point. The reason for their fatal decision was not known since none have revealed their intention in having done it. My present state of mind was in a conflict between the truth of the horror of death advancing in all creations of nature and the beauty of it since all who are born are destined to die. The general Truth down from the Ages was "The soul never dies". It is the body which is disintegrated. The soul lives on and is re-born in another body. The process is repeated till salvation or freedom from the body is achieved. The soul is amalgamated into the eternal everlasting soul.

But can we absorb this without any solidarity. From ancient times Man believed in the presence of a Supreme power's presence in the beauty of Nature's creation. From time immemorial, Man believed God's presence in nature and prayed to the sun, moon, stars, and fire etc. Rituals and sacrifices came at the later stage to please the gods that they saw in nature.

We know man's intelligence far exceeds other creations. Hence the advances in science and technology accelerated to give more comfort and knowledge to the advancement of the human race. But the intellect of man is nothing but a mere spot in comparison to the mystery of the creations of the universe and nature. Hence arose the hypothesis for the existence of a supreme supernatural- One to whom the different Religions have different versions. But it all amounts to the fact that Mankind have tried to impose through different Religions their idea of the existence of God. They have succeeded to a great extent in convincing the majority of the population to believe that it is necessary to adhere to some regulations and practices of their own religion to attain the perfection and nearness to God. Rituals and ceremonies have become so costly in the temples and it is supposed that regularity in its performance pleases God to deliver one from all evil, besides showering His blessings for prosperity and good fortune. Most of the top-level scientists and astronomers have felt the presence of the omnipotent a reality while some have vehemently opposed such an idea. If that is so, the mystery surrounding the order prevailing in the universe and the magnificence of nature's creatures should be unearthed but the puny intelligence of Man has still miles and miles to go before such truth can be unraveled.

Man is the noblest of God's creations and truly the most supreme of all, as he is advancing at a rapid race to be a superman, as Bernard Shaw had rightfully said many years ago. The Mystery of creation and the perfection in the living organs of organism of nature are truly astonishing, unrivalled, unmatched, beyond the capacity of the human intelligence, yet we are unable to identify the real organizer. Such is the way of the Lord for He doesn't want us to know more than what we should know.

As I gazed down from the steep precipice, I felt enthralled by the beauty of the green valley stretching like an enchanted carpet circled round by the divine beauty of the Blue Mountains as far as one would wish for.

Suddenly I turned and asked my uncle,

"What a horror is death! What happens to us after death?"

Startled at my question, he merely stammered,
"Why... why do you ask?"

"I want the truth", I said.

"What truth?"
"The plain truth about death! Death is dreaded, feared. The fear of death has haunted me from childhood."

"Why fear it?" asked my uncle, "When time and death goes hand in hand. Death is a fact and inevitable. We all have to die one day and return to where we have come from. Life is short and the days numbered".

"The fear arises," I said, "Owing to the mystery of what lies beyond the horizon of death."

"That mystery will remain so", said my uncle". "We are limited to time. Death is the end of all and total obliviousness occurs! This is the only Truth that we all can be certain will happen to all of us."

My mind was in turmoil over these thoughts that had

haunted me ever since childhood. My mind now utterly confused with the mystery surrounding me diverted for a moment, my attention to the enjoyment of the huge Blue Mountains towering in front and the peace and serenity attained by a glimpse of the valley stretching far below. The skill with which the zigzag roads had been made through mere steep precipitous is really admirable. To move a short distance, the vehicles had to ply the steep strong winding roads slowly for fear of accidents. The sign "Drive carefully. You only live once" is displayed at different curves to remind the drivers to be alert. It was one of these signs which had re-awakened the un-ending desire to turn the fundamental truth of death which had been haunting me ever since childhood. But in spite of my repeated endeavor to seek the Truth, I was plunged deeper and deeper into darkness and despair.

I was awakened from my thoughts when I heard my uncle calling,

"Hurry! Come on. We have not much time before nightfall".

It was then that I realized that the day was closing. The sky around was clothed in the magnificence of the streaks of golden clouds near the horizon. One wonders at such elegant beauty displayed by the sun, which, while setting turns golden mingled in red color, scattering its colorful rays on the clouds, transforming the sky to such brilliance beyond comparison. The sight is more marvelous when the rays are displayed in millions of scattered streaks of clouds. As I watched the splendor at the approach of dusk, the thoughts of worry and despair in me was deeply affecting me minute by minute. It was forgotten for a moment, and my uncle patted me on the shoulder beckoning me to proceed to the car. Then I was back to my normal state.

Our car sped along the road slowly, the front lights lit as night was fast approaching. Soon I reclined in the back seat and dozed off.

CHAPTER 5 FLICKER OF EARLIER
REMINISCENCE

I woke up to see my father offering a cup of coffee as was his usual habit to signal me to rise from the bed for my usual routine for studies. The nuisance of the ringing of an alarm clock was not necessary as he rarely failed in calling me. His coffee added to the timely execution of the time-chart for studies did a great deal to advance me in my studies.

He always used to say, "Work hard, my dear. You will then achieve the impossible."

I knew that his endless attempt to please my elder sister's husband had succeeded in reducing him to a wretch. Being a prey to her endless pleadings, for money and aid in constructing a grand mansion for her, my father had exhausted his entire savings. Now he felt miserable at the knowledge that he had not much at hand to offer for my welfare. The lack of finance added to the utter indifference of his elder daughter and her husband who had fleeced all that he had, hastened to tear his wretched mind to shreds.

One day he had called me and said,
"My dear, I have had a bitter experience. Your sister has taken everything. The savings for your education too had been withdrawn and utilized for her house construction."

"Now she does not come here anymore, "added my father

47

bitterly. "Her husband sensing that nothing more can be had from us has warned of dire consequences if she is to enter my house again."

"What about the children", "I asked, "Do they come here."

My father sadly replied, "No, they are beaten even if they look my way."

"What!!? I said, "How long since this has occurred."

"When you went to the hostel", "he said, "He keeps telling me that you should be persuaded to drop studies."

"Why does he say that?" I inquired. "He says that girls should not waste their time in studies but be more dutiful at home," said my father. "Much time and money is wasted for no purpose."

"Do you think so, "I asked?

"No, No, my father replied, "You are sure to come up high to my expectations. You rightly deserve all help and guidance" he added, "Your father is a fool that he had been misled by the pecking of your mother who had been the real cause for my present state. I have been a worthless father to you, my dear."

"Don't worry, father, "I said, "I can manage."

The sudden jolt as the vehicle screeched to a halt threw me off balance in my seat and its impact awoke me. The sight of the crowd gathered there in rapt silence was enough to convince me that my father was no more. I hurried past the crowd, my uncle holding me, lest I fall. I tried to take his arms off my shoulders.

"Leave me! Leave me!" But he tightened his grip.

Then I saw him. My father was laid in the floor covered in white except his head exposed for the public view. I felt my body sagging and my legs stiff. Then I stumbled down only to be lifted into the house.

"He is sick. That is all. Why are you people gathered here?"

I started shouting at the people hysterically, and my repeated attempts to wake up my father ended in failure for in my confused stage I did not realize that he was a corpse, body and flesh on the verge of a foul stinking smell given out in the process of decaying.

The people were rather relieved at my arrival for there were differences of opinion between them as to the duration, a decaying corpse should be kept before cremation.

It was then that I saw my mother huddled in a corner with my sister.

"Oh! Mother!" I exclaimed, "See him, his eyes are open but he doesn't move."

"Alas! All is lost, my child", She said, embracing me. "Our strength, our bread-earner is gone; we are now helpless and abandoned in this cruel world."

"No, no, it cannot be", I pleaded. "There is still hope. Pray and start praying for a miracle to happen".

"Impossible, dear", my mother said, "Fate has decided other way. He is gone far beyond our clutches. Perhaps he sees us but far, far beyond our reach".

49

Hindus generally perform and complete the holy religious ritual on the corpse before cremation. There is a belief that this will accelerate the union of the soul with god. One by one the closest relative lined up to accomplish the ritual at the guidance of a priest. As soon as it was over, the dead body was carried by its dearest ones to the cremation place where logs of wood are kept ready for burning.

As the body was taken, I could not control my sorrow that finally burst into uncontrollable, endless pouring of tears down my swollen red eyes. My mother and sister were equally sorrow-stricken and a large member of friends and relatives were engaged in the task of consoling which seemed endless from our nearest relatives who feigned what they did not feel. Why should I blame them for how could they feel what we felt?

For a flicker of a moment, I chanced to look outside. There stood his majesty my brother-in-law smiling and from his unflinching gaze towards me seemed to say,

"Don't worry, Darling! You have me now. I will take extra care of you".

I knew the rogue and the thought of dependence on him was unbearable. I thought to myself,
"Don't be too sure, fool! I would rather die than cringe toward you for support".

But he knew he had the trump cards. He was the one to whom mother hung for support.

I heard her say to him", you have a duty to us. Arrange everything for the attainment of eternal bliss for my departed husband".

He nodded in approval to my mother's words. I knew that he would never use his money but would try to fleece the meager balance of cash left in mother's account.

When my mother came beside me, I asked, ""You have to follow the convention and customs society has imposed on us all from the ages".

"Definitely, my dear, don't you want your father to be eternally free".

"But, mother, do you think that only if we follow the practices which have been performed unquestionably for the betterment of the soul, he can be united with the universal Divine power."

"That is so, dear, we do what the majority follows. There is a belief that these rich and costly rites should be performed for the departed soul to reach the utopia of the eternal bliss."

"What about those who dies unwept and no one to mourn for", I asked, "Those whose bodies are unclaimed or unknown. When no relatives come to take possession, the bodies are in the mortuary, from there it is passed to the medicos to be cut and sliced up to study the practical human anatomy. Do these unfortunate ones do not reach God?"

"I am afraid that I do not know," my mother said, "We follow what our religion teaches. Society would condemn us if we do otherwise.

"But, "I said, "I see the other way. Society has blinded us that we are still deeply immersed in superstitious and traditions. We are living in a fast advancing scientific age. I feel that we are cheated and tricked by some godly men who

51

pretend to exhibit supernatural powers and are able to convince and bring into their fold a huge multitude of people by trickery. We read with shock and alarm the startling sensation caused by some fake godly men who had managed to catapult the crowd, even the foreigners. I feel that they are the ones who outnumber the locals at the ashram. I have read how some of these sadhus who roam about naked and under the guise of godliness, indulge in moral degradation."

"Don't say such things, dear, and "said my mother." It is true that there are some who tends to retreat from the thorny path of seekers of Truth."

"But there are many who, like flashing rays of hope awaken the soul of man to follow the path of Truth."

"Stop this nonsense, "my mother continued, "let us see what Madhu has to say."

"Who is this Madhu," I enquired.
"What?" Do you mean to say that you do not know your brother-in-law"?

"Oh! He…. I am sorry, mother; I really do not place the least value on his person."

"He is your sister's husband. Moreover, he is the bread-earner of our family now."

"My foot!" I spat out." It would be better to beg for our bread from door to door. Our religious scriptures say 'Material and worldly bliss does not bring eternal joy. Hence cast them away, seek spiritual bliss.' We know these spiritual seekers actually begged for their bread. In Ancient times begging and giving was an act of God"

"Do you mean that you would beg now, "My mother asked anxiously?

"No, mother, Society has changed. If we follow the traditional method, society would sneer at our existence. 'Those who have" prevails while 'those who haven't" finds no place in this world infested with rogues, killers, cheaters, rapists and the like personalities. This is the Kali Yugam as has been prophesized. Man has descended into the deepest hell of his existence.

"Allow me then to present an astonishing revelation of a totally hypocritical brutal character of your son-in-law. Several attempts have been made by him to persuade me to fall for his immoral advances but I had evaded his lecherous approaches which show his not-too-good intentions. One day discerning my presence nearby, unmindful of it, he lifted up his dhoti to exhibit his manual desire for a brief moment. I was stunned beyond belief as no undergarment was visible. The stunt was repeated to drive home the meaning of what was conveyed straight to the target. I looked away hating him for having placed me on a footing with a female waving for sexual pleasure".

"Tut-Tut- my dear, you may have formed a false discern of his character. There may be a possibility that your presence there was not felt- you should be careful that the accusation leveled by you should be consolidated with solid proof."

"Mother, besides there are more, on several nights a light tapping at my bedroom had aroused my curiosity to investigate through the peep-hole. Who do you I saw? My sister's husband was playing the night's truant. Tell me, mother, should I hold in high esteem such a disgusting person as he."

"Then who do we turn to for support" my mother implored helplessly.

"Let us hope that there is a God- I replied, "We are bound by Destiny. We can't buck fate, can we, mother."

"If you get a job, we can pull on, can't we?" questioned Mother." A first class degree in literature- you stand a good chance to get a job".

"No, mother," I protested. "Political influence and money stand to gain a lot for influential people, but for a miserable poverty-stricken female, an opportunity in the employment market is bleak."

"Why do you say that?" my mother pleaded. "You have a First class master's degree in English. Besides you are just about to complete your Bachelor in Education."
"Let us see," I remarked, "We never know what life has in store for us."

My mind diverted for a moment to the calamity many unfortunate ones encounter when they run from pillar to pillar for employment gaining nothing but misery and total depression, for those at the Interview Board are total hypocrites and cheats who recruit people through the back-door fattening their purses with the riches of the highest bidders. The Interview is just a farce to eyewash the public. It was not at all surprising when I felt my hopes shattered after having attended an interview for the post of high school teachers for private-owned management schools.

As I entered the hall I saw at least hundred candidates seated waiting, knowing that there were only five general vacancies, and three other caste reservations, my mind was pondering that this was too much of a crowd-unless the whole procedure was merely a show and mockery hiding the fact that the candidates were already chosen while these conflicting thoughts were racing in my mind I heard my name being called. Uneasy at first but then gathering up courage merely strode into the room acknowledging the presence of six gentlemen seated inside.

"Good morning, sirs," I politely stammered out.

"Please be seated" said one Interviewer. "Thank you gentlemen," I said after being seated. "So you are a PG holder in English Literature, Is this your first interview".

"Yes, sir", I replied.

"Have you got any experience in teaching", asked another gentleman. "Sir, I believe I have been trained to teach while I studied for my Bed. Moreover I have an aptitude for a teaching career."

What amused me was the fact that an interviewer who had been eyeing me with an intense sexy pleasure finally managed to blubber out, "what an admirable shape"!

An embarrassment was seen among his co-partners at such stupidity. Not bothered about others, he continued,

"Hey! Where did you learn to do such a beauteous make-up"?

"I beg your pardon, sir," I pointed out, "Do you mean my personal appearance. It is really astonishing that you could link natural appearance with a beauty parlor. The truth is that I do not have money for such extravagance should be mentioned."

The others sensed that their co-accomplice totally blinded and infatuated by my sensuous   beauty may resort to foolishness beyond repair. Hence one of them took the liberty to rise up in his seat and exploded,
"Enough! The time allotted has expired. Hence good day! Miss, you may go".

"Good day, sirs", I mentioned rising up.

Then I quickly left the room in a hurry trying to suppress the emotion and anger which I could control no longer.

CHAPTER 6 FORTUNE FAVOURS THE BRAVE

A new world of Adventure rose on the horizon as I chanced to see an Advertisement in a leading daily. "Qualified teachers required to teach English, Maths, Science, and Social Sciences for senior Secondary schools in Ethiopia. Client will be in town for two days. Rush in for interview".

I read and re-read. Finally a worldly light of hope dawned in my mind. The opportunity is too good to miss for a person like me, neglected and totally devoid of ripe opportunities at the domestic circle, encircled as it is in a hypocritical and corrupted society where job opportunities exist for the highest bidder. Being born in a high caste family added to increase the depression as reservations for backward communities mounted higher than was expected thus robbing the high castes of their deserved seats. No longer is there justification for clamoring for government service unless he belongs to the backward community labeled by the ambitious politicians, over smart in hoodwinking the populace to vote for the party they represent to fulfill their self-seeking ambitions.

Alas! Indeed! A deplorable state our motherland has shrunk infested with self-seekers as politicians, murderers, hypocrites- their ultimate motive grabbing power and money for their selfish ambitions. Patriotism is long dead and eclipsed as Sanskrit had become a dead language to this world. They fool the electors and when they hold the reins, ransack the country to ransom. Even the people who elected them are helpless, mere mute spectators watching the whole show-indecisive, helpless. One truth clearly dawned on my mind Money! Money is the ultimate reality to get insured for a living. Without it we are cast off, neglected by the society we live with. Even our relatives closest though they may be utterly abhor our presence.

It so happened my mother and I were lodged in Sita's house. As our stay for two months was uninterrupted by any nasty scenes, my mother thought to prolong our stay for more time till her grief for her departed husband has dwindled with the passage of time. I believe that destiny holds the reins in our life and we are helpless in its powerful grip.

I felt that I could no longer endure the hardships that my mother and I faced while we were put up with my sister. She seems to have no hold over her husband who always appeared to abuse her in the strongest terms to show his disgust at our staying there. But where could we go for we had nowhere else to turn to for a living. Naturally I decided to test the opportunity that had presented itself suddenly.

I decided to take the next train to Bombay to attend the Interview. Though I had never been to this metropolitan city before, I decided to take the risk. Strange things have been reported about this city where unsuspecting innocent girls are lured by false promises and forcibly dragged to the whore houses to be sexually abused. Most of the victims are from the lower strata of society where the girls are uneducated who are easily trapped into believing that a better life waited for them in Bombay. Only at the last moment they realize that they have been led to a situation from where they could never escape. Bombay seems to be the worst place for women and girls to walk around unless they are fully aware of the streets and places around. There have been instances when unsuspecting school girls have been carried away by men appearing in closed vans. They show utter disregard for the pleadings and the fright shown by the victims. Such situations end either in the death of the unfortunate girls after mercilessly raping them. The cruelty and the inhuman treatment over ladies are occurring continuously in many other cites as the government has failed to enforce severe punishment for these culprits.

But I believe all these mishaps could be challenged if all the girls and women are educated. Then the Government could be pressurized to deal effectively with all the unfortunate incidents which are happening to the ladies all over the country.

But my mind was not at all perturbed by all these thoughts since I felt that I was quite capable of protecting myself if the need for it arises. As I boarded the train and sat in a reserved compartment, I felt quite relaxed and felt that chance may reward me for the opportunity that I was ready to face in spite of heavy odds.

As I reached Bombay railway station, I was totally exhilarated by the immense size of the station. I noticed that the people were rushing past as if time was too precious. Hindi was spoken by everyone even the coolies who rushed along carrying loads of luggage. Besides, the hurry-burry of the restaurant boys and men hurrying around trying to sell eatables to the passengers in the train was indeed a comfort for those who wanted them urgently. The platform was thronging with people who arrived here from different parts of the country engaged in a variety of business. The majority of the people were freely conversing in Hindi as though as they were natives of the place. It seems a pity that I could not speak the language even though I could understand what they were saying. But I was able to manage as I could converse in English.

I approached one of the passer-by and asked, "Could you please tell me how I can reach hotel Ambassador?"

"You can take a private taxi there. There are plenty available at the entrance of the railway station."

So I had no difficulty hiring a taxi as he himself came forward and assisted me in getting one.

As I approached the hotel, the sight of the candidates assembled there shattered all the hopes within me. But having come a long way, my mind was resolved to see it through. The Hotel "Ambassador" was a five-star hotel-magnificent and majestic- a right spot for the top brass and billionaires. I registered my name by filling my bio-data which I handed over at the counter for onward transmission to the delegates at the Interview Board.

It was a long time before I was called. Most of the candidates screened were rejected down- right. I believe that I was one among those who were selected.

I rushed home by the next train   to inform the good news to my mother. But she felt that the path I had taken was totally blind of reason. She was right because society would not approve of a woman plunging to a world of adventure in an unknown land.

I comforted my mother by saying, "If society is so concerned for my welfare, why do they close the doors of opportunity for many an opportunistic youths and ladies."

"But my daughter, on your return to this native land, no

eligible bachelor would accept your hand."

"Hang the bastards! I myself would refuse to be betrothed to such un-intelligible males who think they can fool around with any females or seek adventures in strange lands while denying these rights to the females."

"But my dear, "You know the custom we have been accustomed. Public would not approve of a woman like you venturing into the unknown-lonely and forlorn."

. "Mother, I said, 'you seem to live a hundred years backward. My decision is final and irrevocable.'

"All right! Mother exclaimed, "You are your best judge."

The day dawned like any other day but with a difference. The thought that I had to leave my mother for unknown pastures, the duration unpredictable and lengthy made me uneasy. But I braved such emotional stress by appearing gay and lively as if something astounding had occurred to catapult me to a life of unimaginable happiness. My mother seeing me so happy put on a presentational facial expression which I could see was forced on her countenance.
Leaving her in the care of my sister, I left them without a cry.

MY FIRST FLIGHT

As I boarded the flight to Bombay, a sudden excitement overwhelmed my senses. It was my first flight and you could easily imagine the excitement which was rising within me. It all appeared as a dream- first flight on an Airbus. So immensely huge in size in comparison to the tiny plane I often used to see in the distant sky from the ground. My vision could not fathom the contrast seen in the majestic aircraft then.

As I seated myself inside the Aircraft, I felt so comfortable and relaxed at the side seat. As many as two hundred and fifty passengers were accommodated in this huge marvel.

The announcement was sounded for the take-off. Within no time, the doors were locked. I felt fascinated by the way the airhostess delivered a brief lecture on precautions to be taken on flight.

From the side glass view I could see the plane taxiing slowly along the run- away. Then it stopped for a moment. I fastened the seat belt around me. Suddenly I felt the plane speeding the run away at an astonishing super speed-faster and faster. The next moment some power had lifted me higher and higher till the ground, buildings, trees were mere specks far below. The sight that birds have while on flight was clearly imaginable. A bird's view indeed, it was in its originality.

Fluency in English had given me an edge over the other candidates. Now it was advantageous in the sense I could easily communicate with others and get things done. Ethiopian Airlines had reserved a room at a five-star hotel in Bombay. On my arrival at Bombay I got in a taxi.

"Take me to Holiday Inn," I instructed the taxi-driver. Being pre-paid by Ethiopian Airlines, I paid nothing.
The room at the hotel was well-furnished with all modern amenities. Bell-boys & girls were ever ready at service on call. The meal served was so tasty I consumed a great deal more than necessary.

I believe the Airlines had planned well. At exactly 13 hours in the early morning, I was roused from a deep sleep by a call to get ready, as the next flight was at 14 hours in the morning. The flight to Addis Ababa in Ethiopian Airlines took six long hours. Seeing the beautiful hostess' I felt a deep desire to be one among them. An empty seat beside me, I beckoned to an Airhostess to keep me company.

"Miss," I called "Just a minute."

 "Yes, May I help you"

"Sure, "I said, "I need a company."

"Just for ten minutes."

"Miss, I admire you and your profession. Do you think I stand a chance to be selected as an airhostess in your profession?"

"Yes, if you try, you have the physical structure and height."
"Are you happy?"

"Definitely and are you on a sight-seeing tour?

"No, this is my first assignment as a teacher in your country."

"Splendid! You are lucky. Teachers are respected above others."

"You are lightly clothed," continued she, "Ethiopia is a highly mountainous region cold to the extreme at some places. You should wear woolen clothes."

"I was not aware of that," I remarked.

"Then buy a woolen overcoat on your arrival at the Airport" She said, "It is a wonderful country and you'd simply love to continue here."

"Do you really mean it? I exclaimed," In what sense could I appreciate being here."

"The Ethiopians are kind people and Hind Teachers are respected." She said.

"You mean" I said, "That your people love the Indian Teachers".

"yeah" she said," they simply love the Indians."

"I'm really flattered to hear you say so." I remarked.

"O.K." said the Airhostess, "I must resume my duties now, Wish you all the best."

"Thank you for keeping me company", I said.

ETHIOPIA – THE LAND OF BACHELOR'S PARADISE

On arrival at the Airport, I felt a severe cold enveloping through my body, the likeness of which I had never experienced before. Before the flight had landed at the airport, I was enthralled by the sight from the side- seat. We were about to land in a country surrounded by the seemingly blue mountains on all sides. On landing, I found that the cold temperature was more than a menace than was related. The people there were all attired in thick woolen clothing while I wore a loose thin blouse and sari. If something was not done immediately, my body would freeze and become numb.

A person was seen walking towards me, a tall heavily built man clothed in full suit. I could see that he showed surprise.

"You have no overcoat, Miss."

I ignored him and pretended not to have heard his remark.

He repeated, "Miss, Excuse me,

I am from the Ministry of Education." That brought me to look at him. "Are you from India", he continued.

"Yes", I said
"Then come along, I have come to fetch you to the Ministry".

At the Ministry a lot of Indian teachers were seated. Seeking their help, I borrowed an overcoat. The Moment I had worn it, a surge of warmth over- flooded within me making me comfortable.

I was lodged by the Ministry in a decent hotel "Awraris."

The next day when I reached the Ministry of Education, I found that the large spacious room was over-packed with Teachers who had come to report to the Ministry.

As we sat down in the comfortable cushioned seats meant for special visitors, a spokesman, Mr.Eagus said, "You will be send to different schools at different part of the country in about two days- time .So you have the time to yourself for sight-seeing."

Food was served to us at lunch time. My aversion to their food was noticed by the Ministry. Injera served with Dorowath was the tastiest food for Ethiopians. Kaiwath (meat half cooked) was an additional favorite in their recipe.

The Ethiopians were surprised that their favorite dishes were not appreciated. Several attempts made to relish their food ended in failure. The moment I tasted it, nothing sensational occurred. Finally, I had to be content with the Bakery products, cakes and dried bread and milk served with tea.

How long could I continue on cakes and milk? The truth dawned on me that these items are only available in Addis Ababa. My posting could well be in a far remote area where my survival depends on the native's food.

Addis Ababa, the capital is not vast in the sense it can be easily traversed by taxi. Taxis ply through the highway from early morn till late at night. The fare is so cheap that the people use taxis more frequently daily. One does not have to hire one but as they race down the road, the public could mount on them in between points   and get off as they like at different points giving a mere pittance as payment to the driver.

No distinction is seen among males and females. As I got in a taxi from Arat- kilo some gentlemen got in beside me. No embarrassment was noted from them as seen in my home town. The Men were extremely polite but it was safer to keep a distance as their culture and habits were different.

The Men and women generally lived for the present. Planning for the future was a thing they ignored. They believe that life was for enjoying. Stress, worry was absent from their daily calendar. The Men and women after work spent the time in bars attached brothels where till late at night, they got drunk. It was uncommon for a woman not to have had adulterous affairs with a lot of male partners they had contacts.

The second day of my arrival at the city at the dead of night, I was roused from my sleep by whisperings and bumping sounds at the next bedroom. It appeared as if a lady was crying and begging.

Out of curiosity I got out of my bedroom and ventured to see through the door-hole knowing that the attempt was impolite. I saw two men completely nude. Below them the lady laid, legs apart naked.

The whole scene shocked me beyond my imagination. Such immorality was a common occurrence on all nights at bar-hotels- unimaginable in India where such obscenity and adultery was unheard of among decent folks. Family attachment was often estranged owing to the absence of love and affection for a single partner. Children growing up in such set-up naturally imitated their parents. It was not an uncommon sight to see them indulging in free sex in the bushes or overgrown bushes wherever the opportunity arose.

The most surprising fact is that students did not show the least fear when detected by the elders. For them it was the laws of Nature-to enjoy and satisfy their sexual desire when it arose. No particular love was attached to a single partner by either sex. The students experienced the preference for a variety of sexual partners.

The girls were gentle and lovable. But Adultery had become their culture. Virginity was totally absent. Girls and women shed their virginity without the least botheration of even washing it after the event for scarcity of water. Water is so scarce that even a drop is not available to clean the bum or anus after one shit in the latrine. Toilet papers are abundant for such usage. A wonder indeed that with such immoral activities in unclean filthy smelling vaginas, dreaded diseases like syphilis did not arise for the simple reason that nature provides the protecting cover and immunity. The men and women never took a bath, rarely brushed their teeth but picked the remnants with a pick after meals. The truth flashes on us that with all our brushing, cleaning and utmost care of our body, we are tormented by a multitude of diseases and mental disorders. But these people live with nature, are fed by nature and protected by nature. Health is their wealth. The future has no meaning for them. It is the present that matters. Stress and mental strain that invades us ushers a host of unpleasant intruders that forces an unwelcome entry by which our bodies are destroyed beyond repair.

My posting in a secondary school.

They were compassionate towards me when the postings were done. My destination was Bahar Dhar, a lovely place I was told. Flight was available and my ticket confirmed.

The flight by a small domestic aircraft carrying twelve passengers on board carries all the thrill for an adventure one could yearn for. The continuous tossing and swaying of the aircraft with the droning of the engine made me sick. In spite of the uneasiness that I felt, the sight of the beautiful valley adorned by large stretches of fields with colorful flowers all around made me tingle with excitement. The vast expanse of Blue Mountains towering above the valley was a wonder to behold.

On my arrival at Bahar Dhar, I experienced a pleasant surprise at the sight of the D.E.O. himself perfectly attired in V.I.P. suit advancing to greet me in gentlemanly fashion,

"Welcome, a pleasant journey, I believe", he said.

"Thank you, Sir", A beautiful country too, I must add", I remarked.

"Sure, Sure! There is more to it than meet the eye", he added.

"Are there Indians here" I asked.

"Not many but sufficient enough to give company".

"What about my quarters?"

"It has been arranged".

I was shown to my lodging. More perfect than I could have imagined, well- furnished in the sense that all Modern facilities were available. The hospitality the Ethiopians offered were to the extreme. A maid well acquainted in cooking Indian dishes aided me in the domestic circle. I truly appreciated the sincerity displayed by the maid. The nature to please and satisfy inherent in them truly deserve to be praised.

At school the Director engaged me to handle the 11th & 12th Grade. Lesson plan before the classes was a must. The service of Inspectors to ensure the smooth functioning of Education was stressed upon. Periodical inspection by Ministry teams speeded the system. Teachers took heavy loads and students benefited at a rapid pace.

A Herculean task it was to teach English. So thoroughly backward they were on Grammar and disinterested in English as an alien language. The Director had said,

69

"A good teacher interests the students". "So teach them anything. But first excite them. Then teach".

These words actually accentuated me to achieve a grand success

The State was interested in boosting up the education of the children so that a perfect bright future seemed to be a reality. The utmost priority was given to promote Education to the children. The desired target of the State was to promote better citizens for the State.

The surprising fact which had distressed me was the aversion of Indians who had refused to acknowledge my presence till late in the evening. I had merely nodded on seeing them at school. Since none ventured to greet me, I kept a safe distance from them. Of course, the sole reason for their aloofness I imagined was their reluctance to give me any assistance I may require. It would not be long before they would come flocking when I was properly lodged.

Not at all surprising, these Indian Teachers started pouring in exhibiting pretentious manners by falsification of their true nature. One could not detect the insincerity displayed by them as one is easily flattered by their noble approach.

Mariamma exclaimed, "Well! Well! Welcome!! I am a Keralite. Sorry I could not meet you sooner. "Oh! Please be seated."

How long since you were here?" I asked,

"Three years and I hope to renew the contract", said Mariamma.

"How is life here? Are the Ethiopians adjustable to your needs"? I asked.

"More helpful than you can imagine", "but added

Mariam, "Be careful not to have much contact."

"Why do you say so", I enquired.

"Refuse their drinks or beer if invited. Accepting may be taken as a signal you are ready for sexual intercourse with them".

"What", I exclaimed alarmed.

"Do they think one would stoop to such immoral sexual degradation"?

"Are you married? You seem to be of such a tender age as devoid of the deep understanding of matured adults".

"I am still single", I replied, "The nuptial bliss is still a far cry".

An uneasy feeling reflected from the past.

My mind was fully absorbed in the joy of hope which had penetrated into my whole being that it had no room for other thoughts. One thing only mattered -to acquire wealth. Money is the power to happiness. There is only one truth in the world in this new millennium. Money is essential for survival- its value always recognized by society.

The Plain Truth- My Native Land deeply immersed in the paws of the power crazy politicians who cringes before multi-billionaires for amassing unaccountable wealth or stealthily emptying the government money without a care for their country-men." Money – the unquestionable monarch of the Earth puts all under its heels- the judiciary too are not spared. The power hungry politicians are acquitted of all the heinous crimes they indulge in- more and more crimes, murder, rapes, thrives on the daily news.

The rich are spared of all the treacherous crimes they commit; the poor are mercilessly dragged into iron cells to languish for petty thefts. The Law and Order machinery of the State has become a farce. Justice could not be enforced against corrupted politicians accumulating public wealth for private gain nor on the top brass bureaucrats who are in league with these politicians. India surpasses all in political corruption. Money and power for self-attainment are their sole motive, unmindful, uncaring for the State's welfare.

Justice is denied to those with no political strings or money attached. How ironic and strange!!

The climate being extremely cold covered with dense fog and mist, the use of woolen overcoat became a necessity throughout. At night spring-board beds with foam mattresses covered with thick furry bed sheets were provided for all.

That night I was tucked under the comfortable warmth of the bed. The silence of the night was suddenly broken by the hysterical cries of hyenas as they roamed around the surroundings. As I listened, I was overwhelmed with fright as the presence of two of these fierce nocturnal beasts of prey that were felt in the vicinity. They readily snatched the left-over of predators, crushing the bones of carcasses and gulping them down greedily, a feat un-accomplishable even for their dreaded enemy, the lion. These scavengers crushed and chewed down hard bones cleaning the surroundings of any remnant of flesh and bones that remained left- over.

The impulse to shout overwhelmed me but from my

vocal cords my voice was dead. Repeated attempts proved futile. So I dragged myself into the wide thick blankets covering myself fully in it. The dreaded fear of being alone in an eventuality rang in my senses. Sleep overcame me and I was then oblivious to all the sounds outside.

When I awoke, the cool freezing wind of the night had not died out, but the sky was lighted in a dazzling red.

This was a clear indication of the rising sun though it was not seen, being hidden by the thick fog and mist which enveloped around. The nocturnal beast of prey had sulked back to its dens. The engines of the early morning buses were started and it was a signal for the passengers to board the buses to Addis Ababa and other places. Trips were provided only in the morning since the journey was long and time- consuming, traveling by the steep winding roads through the mountains.

A day at school.

I got up, hurriedly prepared two eggs and coffee for breakfast. Having prepared the lesson plan the previous night, I felt relieved that I was ready for school. The Director had absorbed me for the lessons from 7am till 1 pm. As I set out for school, I covered myself in a woolen coat to ward off the chilly fog and mist. The road was clayey and I had to walk carefully avoiding the slippery sinking clay. The first time I had set out to school, my right foot with an expensive foot- wear had sunk into the clay. No matter how hard I tried to pull up my leg, it would not budge. Finally, some Ethiopians aided me to pull up my leg. The footwear was damaged beyond repair. I was advised to buy the boots available in the market.

These boots being comfortable, I did not experience any further discomfort in walking on the roads.

At school it was all so pleasant. The students, teachers admired me as though I was God-sent. The students of Std. Eleven & Twelve were deadly silent when I took the classes. Rapt attention was observed as though every words of my lecture were digested on them. The mixed class of boys & girls of different ages were more matured and I did not wince whenever the hands and fingers of the boys were lost in the panties or undergarments of the girls, self-seeking, exploring the hidden depths for pleasure. No sense of shame on these playful acts which they seemed to indulge, unmindful of being detected by their elders.

The most distressing fact about the girls, I was told was that their clitoris was cut off at a tender age thereby depriving them of the sexual stimulation or desire. A single male does not fulfill a woman's sexual desire but the thrust of several males'. A sad picture indeed! No wonder they are ever self-seeking for pleasure.

I have often wondered about sex, as I have never experienced one. The fact that I had no knowledge of it was totally absurd but the lack of time to think over such trivial matters as I was struggling to brave the war against fate for survival.

One night a tapping awakened me at my door. The knocking persisted for some time and on observing through the peephole, the figure of a man was clearly visible before me outside.

I shouted, "Who is that?"

"A friend" the voice murmured. "Let us talk and have fun".

"Who are you?" I enquired angrily.
"One of your admirers, the name is Aleymelu".

"Please leave me alone, I am not of the stuff you people believe".

"But let me in and let us get acquainted".

"Not at this time at night", I shouted, "So please clear out or I will call the police".

Immediately he was gone. That night I tossed about in the bed lost in thought.

I had no one to turn to, should a crisis arise. Then I thought to myself that it was safer to play with them but play hard to get. Encourage them but keep them at a distance. They would then come flocking with favors. A country with unimaginable numbers of brothels with bars attached hotels attracted all expatriate Indian bachelors to alcohols and call-girls to enjoy a bachelor's most enjoyable place on Earth where society would not abuse or condemn them. They drank and slept with women, as innumerable opportunities were available in all hotels.

Rather strange!! These very hypocritical Indian bastards seek virgin girls for matrimonial alliance on arrival at their hometown. They have not the least botheration of even declining the marriage, should a gossip is taken up about the bride-to-be.

A few Ethiopian students took me aside.

"Miss, what about your views on marriage"?

For a moment I hesitated, then gathering courage said,
"After a marriage, husband and wife love each other, have children, and bring them up to be useful citizens... They do not indulge in outside sex. Once they do it, marriage is doomed to failure. A husband could never endure the thought of the unlawful entry by others into his partner-for-life nor could his wife".

"Miss, our parents are never together at night. They freely mix with others without the least pretense of being detected".

One of the students said, "Teacher, we would appreciate a single partner-for-life. But circumstances force us to split and seek fresh partners. Society has become like that and we could be only what our society is".

The primitive stage of their culture came to light when at a feast I was invited; I was offered a toast of alcohol with a plate of freshly cut beef uncooked. It looked raw and one wonder how raw meat could easily be relished by these gentlemen and ladies dressed in modern suiting. The Director after much persuasion encouraged me to chew a little. After many kind entreaties and for fear that my refusal would hurt, I chewed a little. The Moment I did, I spat it out, vomiting violently to the utter astonishment of all present. I left the scene immediately without a word, for home.

The next day having decided to go to Addis Ababa to send a draft for my mother, I got up long before daybreak. The frightful laughing cries of the hyenas could be heard. I hurriedly washed, dressed and packed a few things in an air bag. Then I waited, on hearing a tapping at the door, I

76

opened to see a tall boy covered in a long blanket that I had summoned to accompany me to bus-station.

"Miss, Are you ready, it is almost time".

"Sure, Sure", Let us start then", I replied after locking the front door and fastening the lock.

As we trudged through the muddy road, the air was chilly and cold and a hyena was seen eyeing us with curiosity. My companion had a lengthy thick rod which he could use for protection should the predator chance to attack. My body felt a shiver rising all of a sudden as the animal shrieked hysterically limping in steady strides.

"Don't be frightened, miss", the boy remarked. I hurriedly speeded my walk to keep pace with him. Finally, the bus-station was in sight. A number of buses were engine-started, ready for the journey to different destinations. Men & women covered completely in long blankets stood waiting to board the buses.

After thanking the boy, I boarded the one for Addis. As I seated myself, I glanced over at the other passengers. All were clothed in plain country-folk costumes. The blankets, which they covered themselves, were shabby and untidy which appeared to have never been washed for months. Scarcity of water may be the reason for the lack of cleanliness.

Two ladies were occupying the adjacent seats. They seemed amused by my presence. They conversed in Amharic and when I asked them in English, "Are you both for Addis"? They looked embarrassed. From the expression on their faces it dawned on me that they did not know the ABC of English.

Exactly at 6 a.m. the buses started on the mountainous journey. The shutters were all down as it was icy outside. As the bus speeded along the dusty road, the school, the little town, started diminishing from my field of vision to a mere speck on the distant valley as the bus started climbing higher to the dizzy heights of the mountain roads.

At a time when the glory of sunset was to be magnified around the horizon, the capital city Addis Ababa came in sight.

The magnificence of the setting of the sun and dusk was totally eclipsed by the dense fog and mist, which enveloped the atmosphere like the shabby blankets draped by the country-folks.

Ethiopians were proud of their Capital City. They got all what they yearned for here. The endless hotels with bars and women-harlots at their service; the plying of taxis from morn to night at the cheapest rates found anywhere around the world; innumerable banks, clubs and other entertainments provided these people to attain the contentment in this life.

At Markato bus-stand, I boarded a taxi for Piazza, Awarais Hotel. Decent well-furnished rooms with all modern facilities of star-hotels attracted one to the exquisite pleasures of a rich cozy life.

I ordered the waiter to bring me bread-butter and eggs for breakfast. A tray with bread-butter, jam and eggs; mug with milk, coffee, two glasses, and a knife in a large tray was placed on the table beside me.

"Yum-Yum"-delicious!!

The satisfaction I got after the breakfast was unequal in

comparison to the food I had taken in Bahar-Dhar.

I approached the Bank of Ethiopia, a multi-storied building with men and women busy at their work.

"Sir", I asked a man at the counter.

"What can I do for you, Miss", he enquired.

I told him and in a short time I received the draft for Rs.20, 000/- for my mother which I sent by speed post

here. Insert chapter six text here. Insert chapter six text here. Insert chapter six text here. Insert chapter six text here.

The Plot foiled.

In the afternoon, I wandered around Piazza on the look-out for a decent restaurant. The Board "OMAR KHHAYYAM" outside attracted me. On entering I could see Indian families at the different tables. I took an empty table. The waiter came and handed me a menu. The surprise it aroused in me was complete when on perceiving the menu, the list of different Indian dishes could be seen. I ordered Chapatti and Chilly Chicken.

Re-entering my room at Awraris, I could not resist the temptation of the warmth of the bed as I lay on it. I felt as if I was bouncing slightly from the impact of the springs fitted underneath.

The silence in the room was then broken by harsh voices of men in ceaseless whispers in the room next to me. The voices though inaudible from a distance were clear within my hearing. Prompted rather from curiosity, I edged nearer to the wall to over- hear what transpired there.

"Everything should be as planned. A narrow miss is suicide. You should be accurate. No second trial".

"What if we miss the target"?

"That should not be. The Mission is to kill. The target is the President".

"Guards with Machine guns surround him like bees in a live. Suicide trial it is".

"Never falter, suicide attempt through it may be".

: Tomorrow at 4 pm then. Heavily armed soldiers will swarm the Conference hall. The reward is great and promising after".

I felt faint and trembled with fear. The truth clearly intelligible made me stiff. They were plotting to murder the President. How can I warn him? Would he believe me? I wonder? But if nothing was done, my conscience would prick me endlessly.

To warn him of the impending danger would be to invite certain room for suspicion as the President is known to be highly suspicious and dangerous to deal with. Suppose the plotters decide to put off their attempt, it would invite imprisonment followed by execution.

The President's Palace loomed before me. A Majestic building with beautiful lawns, garden adorned with the fragrance of flowers-surrounded by deadly alert soldiers with machine –guns, ready to pounce and destroy any suspicious characters lurking around.

Gathering courage, I approached the soldiers at guard at the gate. "I seek an appointment with the President".

"What for", one of them asked roughly.

"Strictly personal!"

"You can't see him. He sees no one".

"But this is important", I pleaded.

"Get the President on the line then".

They refused to yield to my entreaties. I turned to leave, dejected and troubled.

"Wait, Lady", called out an elderly person with a multitude number of stars on his shirt. The first sight was enough. He was a high official for the soldiers stood at attention on his approach.

"Miss", why do you ask for the President? Say your piece and get it over, he ordered sternly.

"May I know who you are, sir", I requested.

"The General", he replied.

"Oh! Excuse me, would you mind walking a little distance away from these guards".

He followed me to a lonely spot in the garden.

There, I related the whole conversation I overheard. He was stunned beyond belief at the moment and shaken beyond his control.

Holding my hands, he said, "Miss, we will take on from now for any eventually if it arises. The information will be relayed to the President".

Two days later, news flashed around that the President had overthrown an unsuccessful bid at coup d'état by the timely information received from a lady. The culprits numbering fifty desperadoes were executed. The public desired to know the savior. Eritrea, the enemy had unknown spies circling this area and the mission was to have succeeded. A Flicker of moment and luck intervened, I held the trump cards. My timely action saved the day, the President and the Nation. They were grateful-indeed so grateful.

The Reward

I had exhausted the permission from the school Authorities by extending my stay in Addis longer than was necessary. For fear of facing their wrath, I decided to book the domestic flight to Bahar Dhar. A phone call to the ticket Reservation office confirmed a reservation.

The afternoon meal was served downstairs. Cooked rice, fish curry, vegetables half cooked, curd made me feel more at home. How perfect and satisfying I was here.

A sudden speed of activity, soldiers were rushing in with machine guns into the hotel; the hotel Manager stood in attention. Soldiers were taking positions in all places- A mystery baffling all the on- lookers, the cause unrevealed.

The appearance of the General brought to my senses immediate relief. I now knew he came for me.

Hurriedly wiping my hands and mouth with a kerchief, I got up acknowledging his presence.

"The President wants to see you", he declared simply.

"But why? Have I done anything to annoy him?

"No! No! Don't you know that you are the National Hero?

I could not believe what I heard.

Was it real? Absurd! Has the President send his own General to find me. Was I dreaming? No! Yes, it was real!!

I accompanied him in the State's car. A marvelous vehicle befitting a king fitted with T.V., radio, phone and seating capacity for at least ten persons. It was a large car with even toilet facilities. More so it resembles a train coach. I enjoyed the touch of the soft cushion as I lay back on the seat beside the general as we speeded on our way. Soldiers on motor-cycles and jeep accompanied us as convoy before and after the car.

The President's Chamber needs no special description. The Royal Chambers of kings and queens could be identical to the Chamber I was taken. Such magnificence and marvelous construction was a thing of beauty-a fitting wonder of the world. Soldiers armed to the teeth were posted in abundance. As I walked in with the general, they saluted us.

This is too good to be true. A fairy tale unfolded before me. I felt I was transported to a land of fantasy where the inhabitants thought that their queen was ascending the throne to be crowned.

Not much difference! The President rose to greet me. An elderly man in the richest and most expensive suit the country's tailors could stitch, tall and lanky, bearded. He, more or less, resembled the famed Emperor Hailey Selassie, people had known. But this man was different. He appeared gentle but he was known for his ruthless and merciless methods of manslaughter if he was provoked.

"What a surprise", he said gently," I thought of an elderly lady, but you are so young and pretty".

I blushed at the remark, looking down.
"Please be seated. I have got to thank you for saving me".

"But you don't have to, your Excellency", I remarked.

"Let me know more. Tell me about yourself.

"Your Excellency! I am an expatriate Indian teacher in Bahar Dhar".

"But why are you here, then".

"I came to send a draft for my mother. She solely depends on me.

"Oh! Then, how did you come across these plotters".

"The ceaseless whispering voices in the next room made me curious to investigate".

"You are sharp and intelligent.

"I need your services for top level posts. Would you like to continue here for long?"

"Your Excellency, as long as you desire. I like a posting in Addis Ababa."

"Excuse me, a moment please". The President dialed a cellular phone and his voice was authoritative as he said, "Get me the Education Minister on the line".

After a second, he spoke, "Listen, Mebrato, please get me the details of an Indian lady posted as a teacher in Bahar Dhar two months back immediate".

Then he returned to me. "I am just about to offer you a

surprise". I was perplexed and troubled. Why was he phoning the Minister and the Ministry of Education?

Then his cellular phone started buzzing. Taking it, he said,

"Yes, an MA in English with Bed. What more you want. Post her as the Education Officer in Addis."

I was surprised. It was too unimaginable getting a high post for a foreigner. As far as I know, it was incredible. Believe it or not-it was true. The thing was happening to me.

Then he replaced the receiver.

"Miss, you are to be posted as an Education Officer of the Secondary Schools in Ethiopia, soon after you complete a short term Military training for four months. Are you not pleased"?

"Your Excellency, this is too preposterous. This is truth stranger than fiction to me.

"Miss, you can take this as a small gift for the great service you have done for the nation. You may leave for the hotel and await my orders. The payment for your lodging and food are the exclusive privilege of the nation".

The Military training lasted four months, rigorous and strenuous even for woman of my spirit. I was taught the use of pistol, rifle and machine-gun. In the beginning, the awkwardness I felt was later replaced by the skill with which I could draw the pistol and hit the target from a safe distance. Constant practice had its effect and the speed and accuracy with which I could draw and fire a pistol would baffle the westerner if he could see me.

85

Training over, I was posted as Officer of Secondary schools in the Ministry Education. Free-well-furnished accommodation was provided within the vicinity of the office.

In the first week of assuming charge, I invited all the School Inspectors, Directors of different Provinces for a meeting at the Conference Hall.

On the day of the meeting, all the Inspectors, Directors got up as I entered to occupy the chair.

When all were seated I said, "As you all know, the President has placed his trust on me. As Directors you all have a great responsibility. The daily, weekly, monthly lesson-plan of teachers with complete devotion to stick to it to the core should be periodically inspected and the report submitted here".

The Directors and Inspectors felt indignant that such orders should come from a foreigner. But they did not dare to speak as I was the President's nominee. The meeting continued for over two hours with discussion on various topics related to the schools' Management System. Periodical inspection of schools by special squads appointed for the purpose had a spiraling effect on improving the performance of the teachers and schools.

During one of the Inspection tours I made a chance visit without warning. The astonishment and fear of the staff at schools were feasible. Chance encounters with Malaya lee Teachers at these schools; I desisted from making acquainted as it was safer to a keep a distance.

I heard then say often, "She is a Malaya lee, for sure. How she got to the top, none can say".

Gossip travels fast and in record time made attempts to approach me at the centre to redress their grievances but I was adamant in denying them the opportunity to enter my presence.

I was returning from an official tour when I realized that it was getting late. As I raced the Ministry jeep over the plains, my mind was uneasy. I loved driving any four-wheelers and the joy and thrill I experienced was incomparable. But now it was different. Dusk was fast approaching and within minutes the surroundings would be enveloped in darkness-pitch black as the land stretched for miles and miles without a sign of inhabitants and houses. It would be many hours of fast driving before I could reach the town of Addis Ababa.

Night would be frightening and fearful for a lone strange woman as I, inexperienced in a foreign land where nocturnal beasts of prey roamed the fields of grasses and plains at night.

The most dreaded creatures of the night were the hyenas. These carnivores limped along laughing hysterically. The sound would be enough to send a shiver on my spine.

I switched on the light when the road was faintly visible and a flood of light flashed around lighting up the front as I drove along unmindful of the darkness I left behind.

A sudden hysterical cry startled me. Repeated deep howling accompanied the first sound and I was surprised to see a pack of wild hyenas standing right in my path. I pressed my foot on the brakes and the jeep screeched to a halt.

Terrified, the hyenas scattered away from the jeep. But I knew these carnivores were not far. It would be seconds before they would limp around to investigate. I knew I was safe in the jeep as I drove on slowly. On the way I was confronted by foxes and wild dogs. But the noise of the engine of the jeep kept them away at a safe distance.

After some time I had driven past the wild plains. A mountainous road, a steep narrow climb lay before us. I had to be extra cautious as I steered the jeep up the narrow unending curves. It was pitch black around but the light flashing in front revealed a glimpse of a movement at the side of the jeep. After several movements, I was surrounded by baboons-which swarmed outside unable to climb inside as I had closed all the sides.

I drove on unmindful of their presence. After some time I realized I was alone for the silence of the night clearly affirmed it. The solitude and the longing for company made me miserable. It was not for long for the sight that I saw the next moment over whelmed me to a joy of ecstasy. In the far distance innumerable lights dazzling in all directions completely illuminating the city of Addis Ababa appeared in my vision. I had finally reached home.

The Coup d'état

A long un-ending feud over border-disputes had risen in such proportions that a civil war erupted between Ethiopia and Eritrea. Eritreans were calculated in their attempts to overpower a mighty foe and the foxiest, devilish man oeuvres finally gained the day.

On a fateful day, when their enemies unprepared, unguarded at their defense posts were celebrating the night over wine and women, the Eritrean swamped the city and killed and looted the President's Palace guards and soldiers. The surprise was manifested on the Ethiopians who were massacred like a flock of sheep. Heavy fighting broke out in all directions. The destruction of the palace was complete with rapid firing of machine guns, explosions from thrown shells. The Ethiopians had been caught unawares with the incapability to retaliate all of a sudden.

After mass destruction and killing of thousands of troops, the rebels declared themselves victorious. A bloody coup d-teat it was- the dead lay scattered in all directions. It was not known what had become of the President. He may have fled or in captivity.

The Escape

I feared the worst, for the situation had become so inflammable to such a dynamic proportion that, had my past happenings with the Ethiopian President been revealed, my life would be in jeopardy.

I immediately got in line with the Indian Embassy Attaché,

"Sir," I hysterically cried out. "I need help. That also fast".

He replied, "Don't worry! Indians are being evacuated. Within one week all foreigners will be evacuated".

"But, Sir," I said, "In my case, it is different. Slight mistake and I am finished. Most Indians envied the position I held. They may give me away to the enemy".

"In that case, he replied, "You will be evacuated singly. Trust me". I thanked him whole-heartedly on the phone.

I chose to seek asylum in my house fearful of venturing out to escape detection by the watchful eyes of the enemy. Outside the Eritrean Soldiers let loose like mad dogs were on a mad rampage-raping the women and murdering the men as their sadistic pleasures encourage them to hunt down these weak defenseless people as wild animals to satisfy their lust, unmindful of any stiff résistance put forward by their victims. But the wild creatures had a virtue which could shame these murderous devilish soldiers. They killed for food, never for pleasure. Man has been cruel from in- memorable times - hunting for pleasure.

Two weeks passed by and I was oblivious to the happenings outside. A special messenger approached me with instructions to take me to the Airport on an arranged taxi from the Embassy.

"Miss", he requested, "You are to come with me".

The packing of all my belongings had been done well in advance.

"I am ready", I called out to him. He took my suit cases to the taxi and we were on the way to the Airport.

"Is everything O.K.", I enquired.

"Sure, Miss, you don't worry", he comforted me. "Everything has been taken care of".

"Are there many soldiers posted there". I asked in fear.

"Definitely, there are a lot more than you can imagine. But you will pass by as an Expatriate teacher".

"Do they know the spy who had them killed a year ago", I enquired.

90

"They know a lady was responsible but they have not suspected it as an Indian till now".

"Then I may escape", I quietly whispered.

"You will if you keep your head steady", he remarked.

We reached the Airport 30 minutes before the Air India flight was to take off for Bombay. I rushed through the customs unmindful of the watchful eyes of the soldiers who kept guard at all places. My luggage was cleared and my heart was throbbing madly as I was handed the boarding pass.

Then I was seated comfortably on the soft cushioned seat. The sight of the beautiful clothed Airhostess' revived my troubled mind. The turmoil I had suffered for the past weeks seemed to vanish as the majestic plane took off with a roar to the skies.

The Return of the Native was not the same lady who set out for the distant shores three years ago. Now she was rich, owned a two bedroom flat in the heart of the city; had a NRI account of five lakhs. She was respected, admired and her mother was proud that her daughter really cared for her.

Her sister and husband came running at the news of her return. The reunion of the sisters was packed with emotion. Madhu remained in the back eyeing me with curiosity. His children ran towards me, embracing me. I showered gifts for them. Vijay and Minu were immensely pleased at my presentation of foreign dresses displayed before them. The seclusion I had undergone for three long years made me long for the company of dear and near relatives. At my persuasion, my sister was with me for one month.

My brother-in-law had not changed from his former self. I overheard him pester my sister to infatuate me for a loan of 2 lakhs rupees which I readily refused. Instantly aroused at the non-compliance of his request, he started storming in the most abusive deplorable language I have heard. He even degraded me by denouncing in the most vulgar terms; that my hard earned wealth was the result of adultery that did not require sympathetic appreciation. Infuriated by this false misinterpretation of my chastity, the sudden impulse to castigate the wretch was storming in me. Fuming with fury, I managed to keep a cool countenance, eyeing him with sensual pleasure and beckoned to him to come to my room. Noticing such an invitation, he stood amazed that such a change should occur in me. Without the least hesitation, he strode over to my room silently as a cat intends on devouring its prey. No sooner had he entered the room, I locked the room. The next moment the surprise was on him as I caught the wretch by the wrist, and twisted him to a bending position. He started crying out in agony pleading to let him go. But I tightened my vice-like grip.

"Filthy coward! I know not what else to call you!" I whispered to him. "You dare to call me a bitch. If you attempt to do it once more, I have no other alternative other than to bring you down to your senses. The fact that you're my sister's Hus does hold no advantage over me."

He was surprised when I jerked him to one side by laying my hands in a tight stronghold that nearly tripped him.

The military training at Addis Ababa had developed my

arms and legs reflexes that dealing with third grade wretches as the one before me were a flimsy matter. The moment I let him go, he rushed out to escape from what he believed to have been the transformation of Kali, the Goddess who wrecked havoc upon evil-minded demons. The thought of the Goddess lingered in his mind that a dramatic change occurred in him. No longer is he the person I had known him to be but he has changed to become a noble personage I had least dreamed of

PART 2

CHAPTER 7 PROPOSAL FOR MARRIAGE

Proposals for marriage started pouring in from all directions; the news had flashed that I had amassed a great fortune and eligible bachelors spread out their nets to snare the fish within their grasp. In the State of Kerala, the marriage season was a ripe moment to become rich overnight by demanding wealth or wealthy products from the spouse's parents who had to oblige.

In our country the ripe moment for marriage being 21 years for girls, my mother felt that I should agree in selecting a suitable match for myself. At first I was reluctant but I tried my level best to please her by replying to the calls which started pouring in day by day.

The telephone kept ringing continuously.
Lifting the receiver, I enquired, "Hello! This is Smitha, what can I do for you."

"Sure, Smita, your mother, please", he said.

"Why, she is not here at the moment"

"Oh! Then let us talk with each other"

"About what" I enquired.

"I have a son employed as a Sub-Engineer. A marriage proposal if you don't mind"

"Does he have a Technical Degree", I enquired.

"A Polytechnic Diploma. But he is pursuing evening class for a Technical Degree".

"What do you have as demands?" I asked.

"That I will take up with your mother or uncle"
"It does not matter. You can relate it to me. I decide my future."

"My son is gainfully employed. You have to put forward something for your subsistence."

"What do you mean?"

"The amount of money you can offer as dowry, a house, a car and a post graduate qualification."

"What more do you need? Does your son have a technical degree and a house of his own? All he has is a measly sum as salary."

"What!! Do you defy my proposal?" she asked.
"Why not, people like you think that you can live on the profits of the dowry met from the girl's parents. So forget it, good bye!"

At another moment the phone rang, my mother answered

"Hello"

"A marriage   proposal for your daughter", a lady replied.

"Then you can talk with her directly ", she said handing me the phone.

"Holding the receiver,   I enquired, "Smitha speaking, please" I enquired, "smitha speaking, please."

"Mol, "the lady's voice came from the other end, "calling from Alwaye;
My son is working as an Instructor in a Polytechnic College; I would like to propose for him."

"Have you enquired about me" "I asked

"Sure" I would like to proceed further," she replied.

"Do you have any demands?"

"Oh! That subject can be discussed later with your mother."

"That cannot be, you can decide whether you want me for your son or an exorbitant rate as dowry."

"But Mol, you have to follow the customs that society dictates".

"To fatten the purse of would- be groom's parents, I believe", I remarked.

"You are talking off your senses."

"May be," I said   putting down the receiver.

I knew that there was no escape; I was trapped by the phone, numerous calls, endless in number coming from the remotest corners of the state. Calls from Madras, Bangalore, from Engineers of well established Companies pestered me throughout the hours of day. But I did not give in to their preposterous demands of dowry which seemed too ridiculous.

The coming- in of my Man.

Providence places a major role in my life; at the opportune moment something always happens to catapult me away from the customs of these societies that I abhorred.

He came into my life unexpectedly. I had never thought of marriage as yet but there was no escape now as my mother had brought in this proposal.

I first saw him as he walked in with another person. The simplicity of his character was evident in the way he had dressed himself; a plain shirt, loose fitting pants. He was tall, wide at the shoulders, slim at the waist and totally lean of stature.

The first question he had asked me, "Do you feel I am the person for you",

I could hardly answer him at that moment.

97

But it worked out. I was married to him without the exhibition of much splendor and show.

I could clearly visualize the first night with him. I was sitting on the bed in the room furnished for the occasion. He entered silently, closing the door. My mind had been in turmoil unable to comprehend beyond the life of a female gender; never really cared to understand the association of females with males. The most astonishing fact that my husband surmised was that I was shockingly unaware of the basic knowledge of sexual intercourse. His first attempt to embrace and kiss me madly in the lips met with stiff resistance.

He stepped back perplexed and asked, "What have I done, my dear, what any husband would have done".

He cautiously advanced towards me.
"Don't you like me, my dear?"

"I like you", I replied.

Slowly he drew me towards him and kissed me gently on the forehead.
"Dear! It intrigues me that you do not know the ABC of sex."

The moment he touched and caressed my breasts, the sudden spurt in the stiffness of the nipples revealed the rousing of my interest which had been extinguished for an unlimited time.

I could experience an indescribable pleasure inside me. I felt some uneasiness but gradually an exquisite pleasure beyond my imagination overwhelmed me that I held him to me tightly till I felt something rushing out of me.

"Oh! Lord! Praised be the Lord, such pleasure was hidden and unintelligible that I enjoyed it the more now than ever."

Family life in Malaysia

I could clearly discern the magnificence of multicolored illuminated buildings, steady flow of the flashing lights of vehicles as they moved on the over-crowded roads below. These were perceivable from my side seat as our flight was about to land at Kuala Lumpur. The enormous plane landed in the run-away with a thud with the back wheels and speeded along the runaway after landing with the front wheels. The Airhostesses were beautiful ladies, two Malay girls and two Chinese girls. The Chinese airhostesses were attractive though their eyebrow lashes were scantly visible as their Malay counterparts. As they stood up in Namaskar, their clearly discernible smiling features exhibited on their lovely faces had been imprinted in my memory long after I had left them. My husband took me by a hired taxi to a five-star hotel at Kuala Lumpur for the night, a luxurious extravagance befitting a king, with bell boys and waiters, waitresses ever ready to serve at our back and call.

The next day at the rise of dawn, we left by taxi to the outskirts of the city 30 kilometers away. The sight which I saw as we drove through the city was truly amazing. Kuala Lumpur was far better than any of the cities that I have seen in India. The busy roads overflowing with endless numbers of traffic, the tall skyscraper buildings and the multicolored flashing of the different colored lights enthralled me at beholding a sight never seen before. The next moment we had arrived at my husband's flat, a three bedroom spacious furnished flat, I was totally overwhelmed to see the rooms decorated with colorful curtains. Being exhausted, I undressed hurriedly and lay down on the bed to rest my weary legs.

The next moment my husband called out "coffee please". I was astonished as coffee was served by an old maidservant within minutes.

"Who is that? Dear", I enquired.

"Our servant, he replied", she will do all household chores.

"But I do not need anyone", I said simply.

"No matter, she will stay. She had been with me for a long time".

A lot of Indian families lived in the vicinity of the area, I was made the acquaintance of all these people, the males especially were constantly striving to engage in endless conversation with me on the pretext of knowing each other, for I am afraid to reveal it – but there is a magnetic force drawing the male sex towards me wherever I went. My husband had known them for a long time and had been spending extravagantly in their Company that had threatened to extinguish all his bank balance emptying his resources and depriving him of his hard-earned wages which could have been utilized to a fruitful venture.

Things gradually changed on my arrival and I tried to convince him of the cunning maneuvering of his companions. He gave up smoking and become a teetotaler and devoted much of his time in pleasing me in every possible way.

Within a year, I gave birth to a male child. We were overjoyed, the baby was so handsome and kicking and my husband wanted to celebrate a grand feast inviting his friends, families but I refused. I reminded him that he need not be a spendthrift but if he wished, he may distribute sweets for them. "Why don't you suggest a name," I asked. "Well, let me see, what will it be?"

"We will call him Bhaskar, won't we, dear",

"Sure, if that is what you like"

"How cute he is, don't you like him," I asked.

"My God! Like him!! He looks exactly as the carbon imitation of your attractiveness."

"No! No! He resembles you more than me."

"Don't let us argue. He has both our features."

A famous Astrologer, a close friend of my husband had foretold,
"Your son, born in a lucky star Vishakam is destined for great events, wealth, and power immeasurable is foretold of his life time."

I had never considered Astrology as a prophecy of the future. "Do you believe what he said? " I asked "Sure, he pinpoints the truth of the events to come."

"I don't believe man can foretell what God destine."

"But it is a science mastered by a few who predicts by the stars,"

"It still seems mysterious and baffling to me."

"It is wisdom from God, as ancient as our oldest civilization, wonders of science unknown to the masses, but mastered by a selected few."

"But I know many who by their pretensions and false-hood tricks mankind to believe foolishly the unfolding of a marvelous future promised to them."

"It may be true," said my husband. People are easily persuaded and flattered by these hypocrites who are many, who make easy money for a livelihood, thus ridiculing and ------the real ones."

Time passed by swiftly and another son was born after a gap of one year. Even at birth, the child was above normal size, fairly handsome, hands and feet larger than Bhaskar's and white skinned as a sahib. My husband was admiring him when I enquired, "what shall we call him, dear?"

"Prem", he replied. "That is apt as he is symbol of love."

"So shall it be," I replied, accepting his choice.

As the children grew up, I noticed that they were dissimilar to each other as a doe to a lion. The elder appeared so gentle and rarely engaged in quarrels. He shied away from such scenes but the younger one was more active and would intercede if his brother was abused in any way.

Both the children were highly intellectuals and their

teachers stood in awe at their inquisitive thirst for knowledge. Both were inseparable and rarely seen apart. The infatuation for each other bonded them as one. Bhaskar always stood at the top rank in the academic results while his younger brother was not far behind.

Prem often resorted to pranks which landed him in trouble. The teachers were mostly Anglo-Indians and wore short skirts which revealed slightly above the knees. Completely absorbed in correcting the notebooks, a lady teacher did not notice as the students crowded over her with their notebooks in hand. Prem bent down under the desk pretending to look for something. As the teacher's legs were spread out, he stretched out on his right hand a small mirror on which he could perceive the clear image of the hidden part. He was shocked the next moment for his teacher wore nothing underneath. The next moment he was overwhelmed with an electrifying surge of power rushing out from inside him, wetting his underwear. He rushed away to the bathroom and then he realized that he had experienced the joy of manhood.

He wanted to relate this incident to his brother. The mere thought tickled his mind, prodding it to seek more knowledge.
One day he asked his brother, "Have you ever experienced anything out of the ordinary?"

"What do you mean?" he asked.

"Something like wetting of the underwear."

"What! How can you say such things?"

"Why? Is it not natural, Prem said?

"In the night, you mean."

"No! Sometimes, in the morning or occasionally at other times."

"Forget it," his brother replied.
"It happens to everyone at one time or other."

The Annual sports meet was held on a Sunday. The school was decorated with colorful balloons and posters, besides thronging with students, parents and school-girls from a neighboring convent school. Among the athletes assembled, Prem, the star athlete was sure to snatch away the prizes with perfect ease.

At the starter's whistle at the 100 meters, it was amazing to see Prem out-distancing the others without much effort that the spectators were cheering with uncontrollable enthusiasm. Even for the long-distance races, he was able to out-pace the others quite easily thus establishing his superiority over others in Athletics.

Resentment among the students

Gradually his prowess in sports won him wide recognition. The girls of the convent school flocked to him for autographs. He was always seen in the Company of one or two girls which roused the jealousy of those senior boys who were neglected. For them a direct confrontation was unthinkable.

"He has become so popular" said a Chinese student Soon Tai to Kunju, a Malaysian.

"Girls are attracted to him as flies". "Even my girl Aisha shies away from me and follow him" said Ahmed.

"We must do something before we lose our girls," shouted Mehmood.

"Come, let us collect a gang and attack him in the dark."

"OK!" Ahmed said, "But let us think up something. We will challenge him to go to the graveyard at midnight. No one dares to go in such a place at that time. People believe that evil spirits haunt the place.
"Do you want to frighten him?" asked the others.

"Yes," asked Ahmed, "He will accept our challenge. He always boasts that ghosts and evil spirits are mere imagination of the delirious mind."

"What if he accepts the challenge," said Mehmood.

"Then, we will disguise as ghosts," said Ahmed, "and pounce on him in the graveyard."

"Among the grave!! But, should we?" asked Mehmood.

"Why not?" cried Ahmed, "Are you afraid as a child."

"But suppose if evil spirits pop out of the grave," asked Soon Tai.

"Are you mad? How can the dead come back?"

"The dead are believed to haunt the place at that hour."

"If you fear them, you can stay back. I will accomplish it

myself." said Ahmed.

"No! No! We will be with you," they cried out in chorus.

At the school gate, Ahmed saw Prem approaching at a leisurely pace hand in hand with Aisha.

The sight of his girls with Prem roused him ferociously but feigning not to recognize it,
He said, "Prem, can I have a word with you?"

"Sure! Said Prem, "At your pleasure"
At my pleasure, you -----, thought Ahmed.

"Do you fear the devil?" asked Ahmed.

"What do you mean!" exclaimed Prem.

"Oh! It is nothing! My friends challenged that no one has the courage to go the graveyard at midnight and face the devil?"

"And", continued Ahmed,

"I have challenged and betted 500 dollars that only you could do it among all those whom I know."

"But this is quite absurd," said Prem. "How could you be so foolish?"

"I know that you don't fear anything," he said, "I have heard you say several times you don't know what fear is. Fear is natural. Children, women, men, fear the dark. There is none that is born of women who do not tremble at the hideous figure of the devil and demons of hell."

After a moment of hesitation, Prem agreed to do it.

"Tonight at midnight, then," Prem replied and walked away.

The attack in the Graveyard

At dusk the magnificent red ball was fast diminishing and descending down the horizon in the west. After an hour, the sky was enveloped in darkness and the graveyard was totally devoid of light. Pitch blackness everywhere that one would shudder if one were to walk that way.

Three figures were seen by the side of the cemetery. They were deeply absorbed in carrying something and laying the burden by the side. But their attention was suddenly alerted by a slight movement by the roadside.

A boy with his arms round the shoulders of a girl was romancing unaware of the three figures near him.

"Don't be afraid, Aisha" said Prem.

"But why did we come here," asked Aisha. "I am shaking with fear unimaginable. My body trembles as if the devil is here."

"Then come closer to me," said Prem.

He embraced her and drew here face towards him. Her lips

were parted and shivering. He enveloped her kissing her passionately on the lips. Thus they were engrossed when a slight movement behind roused him. Holding her to him, he walked away from the cemetery.

When they were gone, one of the three figures shouted angrily, "The rascal! He has hooked my girl in him."
Raging further, "I will kill him! Will he come back!
"The rogue, if only I can finish him."

"No! No! Exclaimed Mehmood. "You are a fool to take revenge for a girl who cares not for you."

"That is true" said Ahmed. "But we will frighten the hell out of him.
At sharp midnight, the place around the cemetery looked deserted. A loner was seen approaching by the road slowly. The silence and gloominess of the night did not bother or constrain him. When he reached the place, he looked about before entering inside. No humans were known to roam about this place at this hour. Stories were reported by the common people around that vampires roamed about suckling their victims' blood and the very sight of a vampire in a female form was enough to turn anybody's blood turn cold in an instant, draining him dry as a twig. The place has been rumored as a haunt for these she-devils thirsting for blood. No one ventured around at this time even in four-wheelers.

Prem, knowing no fear, boldly entered. Before him lay countless number of graves; he stopped before a newly grave covered and waited with a stick in his hand.

Suddenly as if from Hell, three white hideous

hooded apparitions appeared rising from the graves nearby. Pre-destined doom seemed imminent as they approached with a sinister motive. No sounds emanated from their direction but only rustling movement of the cold wind. The scene was enough to make anyone shudder and collapse, losing their consciousness totally.

But Prem seemed unperturbed and undecided of movement. Then a surge of energy arose in him as the ghosts figures neared. Gripping the stick firmly in his right hand, he aimed a severe blow dashing it on the face of the first grotesque figure. A terrible squealing sound cut arose from it, breaking the deathly silence of the night followed by a thud as it fell violently to the ground. Instantly, the other two figures dashed away before Prem could follow them. The thought of pursuing these ghost-like things were futile as they were believed by many to come from the graves and dissipate into it. When Prem turned, he was shocked to see that the ghost he had struck had vanished. He could not visualize how this could be possible. He could neither see anything as it was so dark. He thought if only he had brought a torch but he hadn't. He slowly walked along the deserted road and finally he came home.

Missing but later found

The next day at school he saw a crowd of students gathered talking excitedly; something awful had occurred. Ahmed's parents were panicky at the disappearance of their son; Ahmed who they said was missing from yesterday night.

The Principal, teachers and students were assembled in the school grounds.
Ahmed's mother was weeping and her swollen red eyes were

still moist as she waited, "My son! Where is he? Please find my son"

"Be calm, Subaida,"

The Principal, a stern authoritative person intervened, "Don't worry, I will find out from the students." He assured the parents that Ahmed would be found soon.

He saw Soon Tai and Mehmood walking away for fear of detection and overcome with a sense of guilt and remorse of the previous night, having abandoned and fled from the cemetery leaving their friend to his fate. He signaled for them to meet him as he detected something mysterious in their behavior.

When they stood before him, and they saw the cane in his hand, they turned pale and started crying, "Sir, please don't whack us. We will tell all." The Principal, surprised at their verbal outburst asked," What!! You know where Ahmed is!"

"Yes, Sir," Mehmood said, "He was with us in the graveyard yesterday night."

"What!" exclaimed the Principal, surprised?
All the others were shocked.
"What were you up to there?"
"He challenged Prem to come there."
"For what?" enquired the others?
Prem who had been listening knew that Ahmed had planned it. Jealousy had made him play his dirty tricks which had boomeranged back to him.
Prem realized that he had struck with his stick. He feared the worst for why was Ahmed missing.

"Sir," Prem cried out to the Principal.

"We should go to the cemetery right now. He may be there."

It was absurd but the possibility that he may be injured cannot be waved aside.

Within a short time all rushed there. The loneliness and the silence that prevailed in the chilly surroundings would unnerve anyone and uproot him off his normal sense.

In the previous night being blinded by the pitch blackness, Prem had seen nothing. But now in the daylight, the graves and the overgrown bushes by their side was clearly visible. One could see that no cleaning, cutting off the overgrown bushes had been done for months. The place looked neglected and desolate except for the lonely graves, a remembrance and final resting place for those who had left us forever. To Prem, it symbolizes the insignificance of man's attempt to hoard land, wealth for his personal greed for power and money. Man is just a pawn at the hands of God who weaves his Destiny. Yet Man's Greed for wealth, power, incite him to heinous actions. Man's life is short, limited, numbered; yet He manipulates his life to achieve his personal ends by hook or by crook. But Alas! The futility of such achievements, all ends in an abrupt end – Death, and the body left in a coffin would decay; worms would eat the decaying putrefied flesh. The skeletons left would splinter to ashes and dust after years.

Prem has read stories of the dead who arose from their graves to terrorize the mortals. He realized suddenly that he was alone. The others had left after realizing that the object of their search was untraceable. Prem knew that the responsibility for the disappearance of Ahmed solely rested on him. He sat down, thinking over his puzzled mind on what had transpired. A rustling sound beside him caused him to tilt his head in time to see rats running underneath followed by a streak and scream from below.

"My god", he thought" The cry seems to be a boy".
"Rushing over, he was stupefied at what he saw. A hole large enough, the depth not visible as the opening was narrow with little width sloping sideways down a narrow passage downwards, the depth unknown. He stooped beside the hole and called out hoarsely, "Ahmed!! Ahm....! Are you there? Ho! There, can you hear me?"

A faint cry emanated from the depths instantly.
Again Prem repeated, "Ahmed! Are you O.K? "

"Please help!! I am dying!

"I can't move", a feeble voice trailed up.

"Hold on! I will fetch help!"

Instantly Prem ran outside covering 2 kilometers to reach a phone booth.
"Hello! The fire station please"

"Yes! Can I help you?"
"This is Prem; please connect me to my father, the Inspector on the line."

A moment's pause, and then,
"Hello! Prem, what is it, my dear," enquired Prem's father.

"Something dreadful, a boy is trapped underneath a deep pit in the graveyard."

"What? Is it the cemetery where Muslims are buried?"

"Yes, Papa. Help is urgently needed to evacuate him." Prem related to him the incident briefly.

"I am coming," his father said and put down the receiver.

Within ten minutes the fire force people reached the scene. After inspecting the pit, one of the men, a rope tied firmly round his waist was lowered slowly down the narrow pit. The other men held on tightly to the rope as he went down further and further. Though narrow, the pit was stretching downwards to a great depth.
Within minutes he brought the boy up, tied to him. Ahmed was ghostly white, shivering with cold, dying of thirst and hunger. It was a miracle that he was still alive. He was rushed to the hospital. His parents were notified. They found their son still in shock over the spine-chilling incident he had experienced the previous night. He knew that if Prem had not found him, he would have been fated to die a dreadful un-ceremonial death.

The next day Prem read the entire episode of the mysterious disappearance of the boy and the final rescue. The Principal was eager for congratulating Prem who had bravely dared to accomplish what no boy of his age could have done. A strange fact was that Ahmed was always seen in Prem's company and they remained as true friends unmindful of the strange enmity that had drawn them apart. "Let bygones be bygones". Said Ahmed.

A dark and a painful moment.

It was on a bright sunny day when nature was flooded with the warmth of the sun's rays penetrating and absorbing the dewdrops that had fallen in the night and the birds chirping

113

happily and the roses and other colorful flowers blooming in the garden below, that I was suddenly distracted by the sound of an ambulance which appeared at the street down below our flat.

The sight of my husband carried in a stretcher by two men caused my over-sensitive senses to be numb and utterly devoid of movement. I wanted to scream and cry out but my tongue- tied state made it impossible for the obstructed sounds to come out.

The men laid my husband on the bed slowly. One of them turned to me, and said quietly,
"Madam, he has had a paralysis, we are sorry. We took him to the hospital but there is nothing else that could be done."
I was thunderstruck when I heard that he had been paralyzed. The tears which overflowed my eyes were uncontrollable; my husband immobile of movement could surmise the depth to which the sorrow of his state had been inflicted on me. His eyes though unmoving was fixed on me, a pitiable condition reflected in his personality which had only a short while before had been full of vitality and life. But now my husband had become a dead log insensitive to movement or life.

My two sons, Bhasker and Prem suddenly threw themselves on my arms and started crying, "Oh! Mother, what happened to our father! Papa, Is he all right?"

I could not utter anything as I knew that their Papa was not going to move again. Thoughts rushed inside me. How kind he has been to me and the children, how much he had loved them all, now he has been reduced to a wreck.
"Oh! Cruel fate, why have you done this to me?" she cried

out.

I sat beside him, wiped his face slowly, a drop of tear fell from his eyelid that was the only movement from him.

Then I bent down slowly and said softly, "My dear, you are still dear to me."

But when I touched him again, I knew that he was no more. My husband had left me forever.

A sea voyage

The sight which Bhaskar beheld was simply astonishing. The Ocean Liner was immense in size and majestic enough to eclipse all other passengers and cargo ships anchored or moored in the Penang harbour. 'The state of Madras' as it was named made its journey weekly between Penang and Madras with a passenger load of over two hundred.

The Malay port was thronging with activities of men and women of all walks of life rushing hither and thither. Coolies engaged in accounting and giving orders, large cranes loading goods for delivery to India which were tightly packed and sealed; sailors returning briskly after shopping in Penang; passengers moving in a line to board the liner; checked by the customs and officials before boarding passes are issued; boarding platform placed in the ship was steep but accessible enough; above all the Captain giving orders in the ship to his men to clear the decks for the ship was ready to sail on this day. The sail to Madras will last seven full days, so the Captain is solely responsible for the safety of his ship and passengers till the arrival to their destination.

Different types of innumerable cabins suited to the

taste of the polished, elite high class; as well as middle class and low class were available. A large dining room with waiters ever ready to serve at your beck and call, delicious delicacies displayed on the tables; gentlemen and ladies eating ravenously with fork and spoons; Chinese gulping meehun with chop-sticks; men and women of English origin draining in their system, Champagne of the highest quality filled to the brim in glasses designed for the purpose; in some corners families to India were consuming bread mixed or spread over with butter, egg omelet and finally washing it down with coffee. This eatable restaurant catered to the needs of those affluent affordable types.

For the middle class and commoners, another restaurant offering all delicacies but with a difference supplied at lower cost. One need not preserve their dignity to eat in a majestic way as many may not be aware of the strange fact that a fresh voyager is easily prone to be affected by sea-sickness throughout the journey with a terrible dislike for food items whatever it may be.

Bhaskar always had a deep fascination for the sea and the ships. The sea in dark blue with the sight of the vast ocean in blue, nothing else all round thrilled him more than the sea. The beauty of the ocean and the sea always catapulted his fantasy to a world of his imagination of satisfaction. The sight of the sea with the tide breakers splashing, rising above to a great height; breaking down with a thunderous roar and rushing down of the foams of the tide with speed to spread out on the shore; repeatedly and endlessly on & on; this feat only need to be marveled at the strength and beauty of nature that is never tired or worn-out; Nature hold out a deep purpose in its endless repeated attempts to pursue a goal.

The sea at times appears so cool and refreshing,

inviting us to marvel at the beauteous creation of nature. Bhaskar have often wondered how it could turn to a mass destruction of Man, shipwrecking ships, sinking fishing boats and men at violent tempests at sea. Sailors, navigators need to be deeply knowledgeable of the changing mood of the winds. Nasty typhoons, hurricanes, tempest had been witnessed by many men in the past. Only a few survived to rewrite the tale of such incidents when the sea had turned out to be a rogue.

Penang Harbour was splendidly awe-inspiring; one would simply be over-awed by the display of innumerous colorful boats, ferries, fishing boats, launches and fast speeding boats flashing past at incredible speed; huge liners of several nations anchored near the wharf; bigger ones and giant liners anchored a great distance away; loading and unloading through boats.

Malays, Chinese, and Indians majority Tamilians were the majority of workers employed as loaders, clerks, and supervisors. Malay was spoken while a few attempted Chinese, others Tamil; while English by the officers.

The hurly-burly was seen from morn till late at night; smuggling was on the rise; goods were checked by customs and confiscation of unlawful entry of goods speeded up and enforced.

The liner they were to sail was anchored close to the wharf. To be precise, the year was 1963, November 24th. In those days, a sea voyage was thrilling and preferable. His mother widowed after living thirteen years in Malaysia chose the sea journey.

They boarded the ship after custom clear-off; their cabin was accommodated to their requirements. Three beds, besides, facing the glass window, the sea and the dock-yard outside were clearly visible. Bhaskar looked through the opening to behold the bustle of people engaged in trade and commerce. Bhaskar's mother still wore the white mourning sari which she had not cast of.

"Mother," Bhaskar said, "Are you not happy to go back."

"No," son, your father still lives in this land."

"Then, why do you go back?" he asked.

"By your uncle's persuasion," she remarked.

"But you should have left one of us here." he continued.

"But your uncle wants us all to go back," she said.

"What of our relatives here," he asked.

"Do they want us here?"

"They pleaded to allow one to stay," she said, "but the show of affection may be pretensions and wishing in their hearts I would decline their overtures."

"We are lucky that you did, that Chettan, Chechi would never like us. They have their own sons. We would become pests in time, "Bhaskar declared. "But, Mother," what have you done with our property and furniture," he continued.

"Chettan agreed to send us the money after disposal," she added.

"My foot," Bhaskar shouted, "He will keep it. We

118

are leaving and how do we know he will keep his word?"

"Let him keep it," she said, "We can't complain, he fed us two months."

"But father helped them a lot," Bhaskar said.

"But that is not accountable for us to say, "She said.

Several times my brother Prem had stiff quarrels with their sons. He had pulled and kicked them; Chechi abused him and scolded him. But still he could not tolerate their high airs. Bhaskar kept a distance away from their adolescence pranks. Naturally he chose to leave them alone.

In Mother's presence, Chettan and chechi chose to be affectionate and lovable to them as to their sons. Nor were they at a disadvantage, for mother had chosen to leave under their charge, the means of getting the assured sum-total of money due from the Government where father had worked, the money Bhaskar was not aware whether it reached mother; the final result of it was a letter received from Chechi and Chettan that father had to go one more year to receive pension, a mere pittance of money was received as the allotted sum and who was there to check the veracity of their statements, thought Bhaskar.

There was neither truth nor justification in their actions. Father had been in Government service for several years in Kuala Lumpur. He had acquired Malaysian citizenship six years before his death. Hence the mystery and untruth was clearly discernible. But they (Bhaskar, Prem) innocent children and mother could do nothing to unravel the truth. They believed them. That was all.

The Ocean Liner started moving slowly out from the Harbour, its horns booming loudly. The sound was audible to us in the Cabin. The endless queues of crowd were waving as the ship sailed out to the depth of the sea. Soon the wharf, people, landscape were dwindling in size. The next one hour, they were completely swallowed up in the vast expanse of the sea and speeding at nautical miles per hour.

They went for lunch in the less costly restaurant. Seated on a table with three chairs, they ordered the waiter for rice, fish curry, egg omelets, and curd. They could see the sea all around them. The sight was ravishing – the sea so deep blue in color – a color, he truly appreciated. The tossing from side to side of the sailing of the ship was mild at first. But now and then the swaying increased that frightened them; but seeing others unmoved, they remained phlegmatic.

Back in the cabin, his brother started exhibiting emotional outbursts of vomiting sensation. Within seconds, he vomited all that he had consumed. The foul smell was certainly stinking. He had complained of an unpleasant sensation in his stomach and a tendency to vomit all the time. His abhorrence of food lasted for several days. Bhaskar chose to stroll along with the deck. The sight of the ship as it majestically ploughed through the unending ocean was too irresistible; at times the sea changed to white, green but the blue carpet of the ocean inspired in him the magnitude of god's natural beauty.

It was a miracle that the constant swaying and tossing of the liner on the waves had not placed Bhaskar at any inconvenience.

Encounter with a stranger

A slight tap on his shoulder made him whirl round. A man well over six feet towered above him. He had a moustache twirled to display a severe countenance. The shoulders were massive and wide and the man was indeed a sailor by profession, besides, his uniform white and a white cap worn on his curly hair, a deep scar outlined on his cheek bones, thick eyebrows, a massive nose revealed his irreconcilable character and his irritable and volatile nature which were confirmed by his intolerable remarks to a lady's polite request.

His intoxication did not bother Bhaskar but it intrigued him at the particular interest placed on him.

"Boy, I, a sailor for many years, I like you, boy. Are you on a holiday going?"

"No, Bhaskar replied, "I am returning to my native land."

"Your family with you," the sailor asked,
"Yes, mother and brother."
"What about father," he asked.

"He is no more," Bhaskar said, "we are returning with his ashes in an urn."
"I am sorry, boy," he replied. "It happens. God is like that. He shuts one way but opens another."
Bhaskar could not comprehend what the sailor meant.
"We are friends," the sailor said, "I will help you. Who comes in Madras, you people alone?"

121

"No," Bhaskar said, "Uncle will come"
Then suddenly the sailor asked, "May I come to see your mother, O.K."

"No," Bhaskar said, "she doesn't like anybody. She does not talk with strangers."

"O.K., then," he said, "we will be friends, O.K." saying this he left hurriedly.
Bhaskar did not relate this incident to his mother. That day he slept soundly in the right. The constant tossing of the ship did not worry them.

The next day he asked the waiter to bring breakfast and lunch to their cabin. They had lost their appetite for food; hence much was not ordered but sufficient to satisfy their appetite.

On the deck Bhaskar saw the sailor approaching at a brisk pace. The sailor came towards him as a most trusted person.
"Boy," he said, "I looking for you from morn, now I, happy."

"Why do you look for me," Bhaskar asked.
"You are my friend. I, do not like to talk to anyone, that's why I talk to you because you are my friend," the sailor said.
"See the sea," he continued, "I have been with the sea for twenty years   I saw many lands. I seek adventures in many lands."

"I too like the sea," Bhaskar remarked, "can you tell me your story, then."
"Sure, sure," the sailor said, "I like you boy, you hear my story."

Threat by the stranger

Then he recounted to Bhaskar a strange tale of pirates, robbers at sea, and his experiences with these cut-throat hooligans at sea; of mutiny at sea and lost treasure; how he has possession of some treasure; his escape from death.

Suddenly he shrieked,
"Boy, I now tell you something. Don't leak it to anyone."

"What is it? Bhaskar enquired anxiously.

"You do me a favor. I have a treasure chest. It's small but it is gold biscuits, small chest with 50 kilos of gold. I got it from a pirate and I" …….. He added venomously, "I killed him."

Bhaskar drew back from him shocked and frightened.

The sailor threateningly added, "Your father's ashes are in a luggage. You take and place my gold in that luggage. Customs will not check your mother's luggage because of the ashes. It is sacred."

"No, no," Bhaskar shouted. "I can't do it, I can't help you."

"You will, boy" he said and approached me menacingly, revealing a pointed knife hidden inside his shirt.

"If you reveal or leak out this, I'll kill you, your mother, "he said venomously.

Bhaskar kept silent, being paralyzed with fear. He had never experienced such an ordeal. The sailor had reiterated

123

that at night he would bring the gold and Bhaskar was threatened to place it in the luggage without his mother's knowledge. Such a trauma he had never experienced before.

As rendezvoused, he came after midnight. Mother and brother were soundly sleeping. Handing over the gold sealed in a box, he cautioned Bhaskar of dire consequences if it was leaked out. Saying so, he left. Silent as a cat, Bhaskar opened the large suitcase and kept this sealed box within the range of the sealed box with the sacred ashes. When it was completed, the loud thumping of his heart stopped. Mother still snored away unaware of what had transpired.

It was highly preposterous that this would not be unearthed by the custom officials. But the threats of the stranger were implanted in Bhaskar's mind and he could not cast aside his warnings as it foretold impending doom.

That night his mind was tortured by conflicting thoughts of an imbecile who had not acted on the spur of the moment. But what could he do? He feared the man who he believed could carry out his threat.

The sudden disappearance of the stranger

No one was seen on the deck as it was past midnight. Bhasker was deeply immersed in his thoughts when the deck was splashed by quick lashes of foams of spray from the waves. For a time he was shaken, inert and undecided. The sea was rough; the deck was splashed over again by the mighty waves. He decided to run back to his cabin.

Suddenly it happened; he heard a dull thud and a loud shriek and a piercing cry; the howling of the wind and the thrashing of the waves deafened the outcry. Some object or person had fallen overboard; of that he was sure; he ran to see near the hull. No one had heard it, he was also uncertain, the howling of the wind and the wild splashing drowned further of what may have been the imagination or instigation of his racing mind. Inability to decide further hastened him to his cabin where he slept unmindful of the incidents of the night.

For the next two days there was no trace of the stranger. His elusiveness baffled Bhasker. Was he trying to avoid meeting him till the ship docks? On the fourth day his absence was incomprehensive and indiscernible as lingering thoughts prodded his mind whether the cries and wailings Bhaskar overheard that night was a connector to the sailor's absence and disappearance. Even if it was, he had to remain phlegmatic since it was fool- hardiness to disclose anything related to that person now as suspicion would boomerang to him; he would be the culprit and criminal for having concealed it then and not revealed it at the precise moment; he could not confide this, not even to mother. He was not at all remorseful or repentant to the sailor's fate.

At night, joyful cries and shouting on the deck below instigated him to investigate. After four days of voyage in the deep sea without a glimpse of land or other people than in our ship, the people were electrified into an ecstasy of joyfulness that could be indescribable on learning that an enormous ship `S.S.Rajula' Liner would be passing very close to their line on its way from Madras to Penang.

All rushed to the deck, the passengers of all cabins awaiting the inevitable. They were fed up with seeing the sea, only sea, the vast expanse of the ocean all round; nothing else they could see; how disgusting; the thoughts of all united in exuberant joy to witness the great event.

Darkness everywhere round the ocean, pitch black that the noise of the breakers and waves only were audible. Suddenly the eye-catching event appeared before them. A remarkably illuminated towering ship lighted with flashing, golden and dazzling lights passed in the opposite direction but so close. People from both sides shouted, waved and cried; some were dancing with glee; others howling and whistling. The incident which lasted only five minutes was indescribable.

The next day at noon there was a commotion on the deck. People flocked to witness a spectacular event. A school of Dolphins had crossed over our path. The stunts of the Dolphins as they lunged from under to a height above the sea, then diving deep below was simply stupendous; diving at an amazing speed and dexterity. Soon the dolphins were left far behind.

Arrival at Madras

On the seventh day, land was sighted as a mere speck in the distance. People started shouting, dancing with emotion. At last the tiresome journey had culminated to the destination – Madras. The Liner steamed its way slowly as the distance between the land and ship diminished.

Madras could boast as a great port. Ships from all over the globe flocked here. Here merchandize arrived from every direction, ships, liners, boats, speed boats, ferries were moored in the wharf. Their ship came within walk able distance and dropped anchor; then pulled to touch the harbour and moored. A platform was lowered to the ship's side; people started disembarking to the Harbour.

For a flicker of a moment, Bhasker's mind was racing when the customs officials questioned them. Handing over a letter to the official from the Malaysian High Commissioner stating the status of mother as returning after the bereavement of her husband which loss is neither irreplaceable and irreparable; maximum care should be taken to let her luggage through as tax-free; the luggage was passed when the identification of the Authority stating the fact of the ashes in the urn was shown. It was a lucky break for if it was discovered, Bhasker would only have blubbered and poor mother unaware of it might have been shocked to death.

As they cleared the customs, their luggage was brought to the exit by coolies. Uncle was there waving to them. Mother on seeing her brother collapsed; the after-effects of untold depression and worry which had goaded her but she had withstood all till she reached her trusted, loving brother. Then her emotions swept her; she swooned and fainted. Uncle held her when she regained consciousness, "It is O.K. girl," he said, "You are with me now. Rest easy and be comfortable."

"It is fate," he continued, "You have to bear it. Be bold. You have your children to look to."

She remained silent and crestfallen. He held Bhasker and Prem to him. Uncle was a god-fearing gentle person whose love for them had no limits; he was not comparable to those relatives in Malaysia who pretended what they did not feel.

He hired a taxi and they were accommodated in a decent hotel.

The next thing Bhasker remembered was that he was in a well-furnished room in a hotel in the Metropolis, Madras; a view from the window revealed a hectic activity of motor-cars, lorries, auto-rickshaws, plying at endless stretch through the hurry roads; Trams packed with people flashed past on the rails. People even traveled by cycle-rickshaws, the only cheapest travel available; pedestrians were seen in large numbers moving like a swarm of ants by the side walk; the expression on their faces revealed a mechanical approach to life; life devoid of the pleasures and enjoyment of nature held sway being influenced by a systematic routine of work and earn from morn till late in the night; they sweated endlessly and a feeling of wretchedness were outlined on their countenance.

In the distance, the sight of the ships, boats, and the ocean glorified his vision, interrupted at times by the thunderous roar of the planes as they majestically soared above the blue clear sky; altogether a hell of activity everywhere.

The room was spacious, three bedrooms bath-attached; call boys ready to please; T.V., phone facilities installed. Superficial arrangements for a posh living; designed well to empty the purse rapidly.

A public school in Madras

Just then, uncle's joyous exuberance vanished from his countenance with a firm resolve to execute a design for the education of Bhasker and Prem who he believed were totally ignorant of the local language, but only well-versed in the English language. It would be undiscriminating if they

128

were to be taken to their native place to continue their education and their future would be undetermined.

"Why don't we try the schools in Madras?" Uncle said, "Education here surpasses our schools at home." "But what about lodgings," Bhaskar's mother enquired.

"That can be taken care of. There are boarding facilities," he said.

The next day in the rush hour they went by taxi to a Christian Boarding School located in the city. On their approach, the Headmaster fully gowned in a priest's robe, greeted them pleasantly; his physical stature so huge and striking to frighten the youngsters under his charge; his voice rough and hands though covered till the wrist showed hairy outgrowth like an ape's. On the table a long slender cane slightly bent was placed to show that he had manipulated it to spank outright innumerable boys to his satisfaction. On seeing Bhasker and his brother, his smiling face lit up to reveal a sadistic thrill for preparedness to whack them brats as he deemed.

Turning to Bhasker, he enquired with grimness, "Boy, how far have you gone in studies?"

"Completed the eleventh grade, Sir," Bhasker replied, then added, "Sorry, Father," reminding him and reverencing his priest's robe.

"What about the other?"

"Tenth grade, father,"

Both of them were interviewed for thirty minutes. Their scintillating answers pleased him. They were admitted to Grade Twelve & Eleven.

The Headmaster accompanied them to the Boarding where they were lodged in a single room. Before leaving, he whispered, "Be careful of the seniors. If they try any pranks, report to me, so saying, he left.

Before uncle and mother bid them farewell, Bhasker turned to mother and said,
"Don't touch father's ashes till we come. The holy dip can be done in the sea at Varkala."

He made sure that the heavily-laden gold that he had secured in his luggage was brought to his room, the key he kept secretly with him. He knew the volatile situation he was facing that was likely to shatter his mind to shredder should the thing be exposed to the public view. His mind uneasy at not having disclosed it, thought it better to relinquish his right to it to confide in his brother. Hearing his story, his brother shouted,

"Why did you hide it from uncle?"

"I was afraid of the consequences?" he said.

"Would you like to see it?"

"No, not now, better you find a safe place to hide it."

"But where?" Bhasker asked. Suddenly an idea flashed and he said, "why not open a locker in the Bank where I have an account and leave it there."

"Then do it at once," said his brother supporting him.

The Manager was overwhelmingly pleased to accede to Bhasker's request as his uncle was a highly influential person and Bankers were at his beck and call. He deposited the gold in the locker, pocketed the key and left untroubled on its account anymore.

Ragging at the hostel

Life at the hostel, he dreaded because of the barbaric ragging undertaken by the seniors on juniors. This menace ought to be extirpated wholly. A senior notorious boy waited at the steps with the others, bullying those boys whom he knew would offer no resistance.

"Hey, you," he called. Bhasker. "Come here," As Bhasker approached the bully named Tommy; he was pinched in the ears. Since he offered no resistance, Tommy became bolder. He pushed Bhasker down the stairs that he nearly fell. Still he did not retaliate but walked away hurriedly. This naturally incited Tommy to pour abuses now and then.

"Stupid rascal," Tommy shouted and jeered," fuck you, you sucker." Bhasker could tolerate these no longer. So he avoided Tommy whenever he could. But for how long? By nature he was quiet but his brother was different.

Once he was strolling with his brother when Tommy with the others confronted them. Intentionally and with a sinister motive, Tommy deliberately shouted, "son of a bitch, where are you headed for?"

Before he could blurt out further, Prem caught him by the

wrist, pulled him and aimed a straight upper cut with his left hand followed by a swift slash with his right wrist. The blow landed with a dull thud straight at Tommy's nose. The next instant, blood started oozing out from his nose and mouth. Screaming, Tommy cried out, "He has killed me." "No," you fool, you are O.K., Prem replied. "You deserved such a hiding."

Crying and folding his nose with his kerchief, Tommy ran to report to the Headmaster.
The Headmaster came running.

"Hey, what is going on?" he shouted.

"Come here," he said to Prem.

"What have you done?" He had Tommy taken to the first-aid room and the cut was bandaged.

Wielding the cane in one hand, he raised it to deliver a blow at Prem.
But Bhasker intervened. "Father," he pleaded. "He called our mother a bitch."

"That so, why?" Father enquired.

"Simply," Bhaskar replied," He used to personally insult me with abuses, threats and blows which I always evaded."

"But now it was different," he continued, "he called my mother names."

Hearing this, Father realized that the fault was not theirs. Hence they were pardoned.
A crowd of students gathered and Prem was turned a hero

from thence. He was nicknamed as Tarzan. His mere presence was enough to turn all raggers to flee. He became so popular that he was elected as the school prefect.

Another striking feature of this school was that nearby a reputed convent – educated institution housing cosmopolitan girls mostly Anglo-Indian origin were housed in it for educability in the western style. The school uniforms of these girls were white blouses tightly fitted with a pink tie, the skirts too short that it exposed the voluptuous thighs and legs. Some even under thirteen were overgrown to women-hood. Ample opportunities existed for the opposite sex for love-making or even flirtations.

LOVE AT FIRST SIGHT

It was by a chance encounter with a group of school girls, Bhasker was enthralled by the piercing gaze of one whose penetrating look seemed to make his body numb. The continuous gazing day by day was totally inconceivable that he was constantly tossing restlessly at nights in the bed. The infatuation for this girl was inexplicable and inextinguishable. He was madly in love and he was considering in his mind how best to approach her.

The opportune moment came as he saw her walking alone by the side of the road and gathering superhuman courage, he approached her foolhardily and blurted out, "My name is Bhasker and what is yours?"

The sudden exhibition of boldness stupefied and astonished her.

"Hello! My name is Anna, "She blurted out.

"Studying in the eleventh, I believe, "he continued...

"Sure, sure, how did you know?"
"I know all about you."

"How, "she asked surprised.

"Because I love you, Anna."

"We will be friends, won't we," he stammered.

She remained silent but scrutinizing her closely, revealed that she was experiencing a similar closeness to him. Admit it or not, it was love, attraction for each other – a magnetic force drawing them closer to each other, unmindful of the passing of time which was not noticed at all.
Suddenly he took her hand in his,

"We will meet again, tomorrow, won't we," he whispered. She nodded.

That night he could not sleep for her face was haunting his mind. It was so pleasant to visualize both of them completely engrossed in love, pouring out their love-sickness to each other.
He could hardly wait to see her again. His mind was tormented with nothing else but about her.

He could see her as if she stood before him. She was tall and magnificent in looks, extremely fair in complexion with not a blemish noticeable. The most striking decoy is her eyes, so luring and cupid-like.
The irresistible desire to see her again was totally uncontrollable to resist.
The next day when he saw her, his mind was jubilant.

"Hi! I am sure glad to see you again."

"Am I late?"

"No, but I was dying to see you."

They started strolling towards the beach which was close-by.
"Are you Irish, "he asked breaking the silence…???"
"Yes, what else you know about me" she replied.
"A lot more," he replied.
She blushed and asked, "Really!"
"Do you doubt it, your luscious lips, tempts me to desperate acts:
"What acts?" She enquired innocently

"Do I have to show you?" he whispered.

He started edging towards her but she kept her ground. When they were close to each other, they stood immobile and undecided of movement.

It was then that the girl moved as if in a daze and clung to him pressing her lips to his softly.
"My Anna," he exclaimed surprised, "what have you done?"

"Why, my love," she said softly,

"Don't you like me?"

Slightly taken back, he said, "I have never experienced it before."

He had really enjoyed the touch of her lips but also shocked at the boldness displayed by his girlfriend.

135

They met regularly and their love-making continued Bhasker seemed to enjoy and derive much pleasure out of the simple romantic love they had for each other; he preferred romancing this way – nothing more.

Selected for higher studies abroad

One day Anna rushed into my room in an excited hysterical state. She was gasping for breath as she had run some distance.

"Oh! My Bhaskar, you are going away."

"What do you mean?" Bhaskar enquired surprised.

"You have been selected for the most prestigious scholarship to study medicine in the University of Scotland."

"My! MY! Bhaskar stammered, "Are you really sure."

"I am damn sure as hell," she said.

"Then we should be happy."

"What do you mean? We! You alone are going away ….. Too…. far from me.
"No! No! My love, do you think I would desert you."

"It is natural. You will forget me and meet new girls."

"No, Anna," Bhaskar whispered holding her to him.

"I can never forget you … never … ever."

"I hope so, "she replied weeping.

Bhaskar held her close to him, caressing her face with his hand, kissing her softly on her eyes to wipe her tears.

"You are my first love but then the only one … ever."

She clung to him raising her face to his. "Bhaskar," she whispered, love me now that I may feel you always in me forever."

"No! No! Anna, my love for you is deep, so deep that you have to wait … that too for some time."

"And," he continued," I will come to claim you as my own."
"It is too good to be true. I doubt it would last."

"Have patience, Anna and wait for me."

So saying he left her happy but her grief was so intense that she was overcome with tears.

Bhasker inspects a soiled map.

As Bhasker withdrew cash from the bank, a sudden impulse to investigate the treasure he had concealed in the locker entered his mind. Making sure that no one was nearby; he opened the locker and opened the casket. At first it would not budge but after forcing open the lock, he was stupefied at the sight of uncountable gold biscuits and gold coins deposited in the box. The sight of the shiny yellow wealth shook him nearly to an amazing wonder. He plunged his hand underneath seeking to feel the precious coins when something oily came within his grasp. Pulling it out, he found a soiled dirty parchment of old paper torn at many places. He pulled it all out, pocketed it; then closed the casket and placed it back in the locker.

In his room the torn papers were pieced together on a table like the fittings of a jig-saw-puzzle. Finally after much trial, he succeeded in piecing the whole picture which really shocked him when he perceived what it revealed. A treasure map indeed, complicated but decipherable. He glued the torn parts, took several hours absorbing the whole map. It took him more than a week to decipher those treasures much beyond the dream of any man which could be coveted from the depth of the ocean. Man in his greed for wealth had plundered, killed robbed wealth and hid them in un-accessible points in the depth of the sea in his haste to escape his enemies, with the sinister motive of returning later to reclaim it. But they failed to turn up as they met their end fatally. The treasure was permanently lost in the sea, unclaimed, lost.

Bhasker, after studying the soiled parched map was able to surmise that some treasures were hidden in the sea near Scotland and folding them neatly he kept it in his suitcase.
The moment he boarded the flight to Scotland, he turned to see his Anna waving to him which he reciprocated. Then he was airborne and there was much thoughts to occupy his mind as the airhostess served food and drinks. He thought of Anna, how dear she was to him but he could not help it. He had to go; life was like that. You have to move when opportunities present themselves or you are lost.

When the plane landed in Scotland International Airport, he woke up with a jerk. It was night; the Airport lighted splendidly illuminating the place like a fairy land. So wonderful it was to see the colorful lighted buildings, giant airliners taking off and landing simultaneously.
At the entrance a well dressed Englishman met him "Are you

Mr.Bhaskar."

"Yes, Sir," he said.

"Then follow me," the man said, "I represent the University." Bhaskar followed him to where a group of students were gathered. These students were the batch selected from India. They were ten in number and they got to know each other. The most striking feature was that the top ten of different schools had been chosen; naturally a stiff competition lay amongst them. They were accommodated two in each room to facilitate in their studies at the University Hostel. The rooms were well-furnished, neat, met all the requirements.

On the first day of lecture in the classroom, the Professor dressed in full suit, bespectacled, bearing an imposing personality in his appearance as a well-established doctor, addressed them smiling, "Good morning, all of you, and welcome to a noble profession. You are just fated to be educated to the most attractive, desirable profession in the world. Be assured that God has chosen you all as his instruments for healing.

The speech continued for one hour and there was rapt silence among the twenty-five students of which ten were girls. Among them Thomas, Balakrishnan, Ashok and Bhaskar were absorbed in taking down notes of the speech of the Professor.

Days passed on, the classes increased at a tremendous pace; the shocking aspect of the class was when they were taken to the operating theatre. Bhaskar was on the verge of absconding when a demonstration was done by tearing open a dead corpse to show the magnificent wonders of a human body.

Thomas held him tightly by the hand and Bhaskar chose to look the other way. But the Professor called him, "Bhasker, don't worry, you will get used to it in time. I know many students who kept away. But they were the ones who later became famous heart-surgeons."

Hearing this, Bhaskar tried to keep with the others. In time, the dread and fear at seeing the bodies sliced open by surgical scissors vanished. After continuous trials at surgical attempts on the corpses lay out on the table, his fear disappeared.

His remarkable progress at studies was glorified when Bhasker overtook the others which were admired by his colleagues and the professors.
Balakrishnan, Thomas stood in awe at the astonishing speed with which their friend Bhaskar could grasp the subjects. As the years passed, Bhaskar scored top marks leaving a wide margin over his colleagues.

One day the Professor David Barlow came and congratulated Bhasker. "Well done! Great achievement! You are selected for higher studies in Medicine in the University of Edinburgh.
Bhaskar felt jubilant, "Doctor, can I specialize in Heart surgery."
"Of course, my boy, you can outshine the others in any field. Do unto Humanity what god has chosen you for."

"Professor, I would do my best for humanity and be an expert as Christian Bernard." Good! May God be with you," so saying, he walked away.

Glorious ascend of one's career

Years passed, Bhasker rose to the soaring heights of glory he has never dreamt of, the lucky star under which he was born was indeed responsible for such an achievement, he established his supremacy in learning in the University of Edinburgh that they chose him for the fellow of the Royal College of Surgeons – a scaling upward to the highest peak that can be attained in medicine.

He was appointed as a Professor at the University and his practice earned him fame within a limited time. Bhasker's repeated successful heart-surgery was recognized by all the doctors. Whenever confusion prevailed in a surgical heart-transplant, he was consulted; his mere presence infused confidence on his colleagues.

Bhasker was kept endlessly busy rushing hither and thither, attending to emergency operations; even performing heart-surgery on alternate days; utter exhaustion was borne on his face by the time he retires to bed; sometimes he has to be awake till late in the night. Nevertheless, Bhasker felt happy; he felt that he was doing something that God has chosen him for.

His over-exhaustion makes him forget his dear ones, his mother, brother and Anna whom he loved still. But he has no time to think of them. They are so far, far away from him ….. Too far away…. he believed…. Even his mind is not free to think of them.

Bhaskar never had a break, was overburdened with patients rushing in for emergencies; he was always at hand, never hesitated to offer his service to anyone in need. Once, when his driver taxiing his car out was suddenly stopped by Bhasker, when he saw a patient in a serious condition carried inside a stretcher. The women beside him weeping were enough to attract his attention.

He got down and in the emergency room checked the

patient. The next moment he called the attendants and nurses. "Get him quickly to the operating theatre and be ready by thirty minutes."

It was a command directed at the nurses and they promptly complied.

When he walked into the theatre, everything was ready. He performed the surgery with such dexterity concentrating on the minutest particles of the human body magnified through the glass he wore. Within twelve hours of strenuous tiring work, he accomplished that which was impossible for many. The successful outcome of the feat was widely acclaimed by his colleagues.

The patient's wife, a middle-aged woman, perfectly fair and slightly above average height, entered the room. Her beaming face indicated the happiness reflected in her.

"Doctor, how can I express my gratitude? You have saved my husband," she said.

"You don't have to," Bhasker replied.

"But," she said, handing him a Cheque, "Accept this as a token of payment.

"No! No!" Your words are enough," Bhasker returned the Cheque.

The next moment, the women fell down at his feet and held on to him weeping bitterly, "you are god-sent for sure; I thank the Lord for you."

Bhaskar lifted her to her feet and comforted her saying, "Look to your husband. He will be completely normal in a few weeks."

Life had its ups & down for Bhasker's mother. On her husband's death, she had experienced the revelation of a tragic moment of utter loneliness and desperation except for the company of her two sons. Her sons had compensated the loss by rising to positions of recognition and renown. Prem has since proved his prowess in Athletics and risen to such heights; he is at present practicing in Patiala for excelling in Beijing Olympics. He has amassed innumerable medals, trophies in National, Asian and commonwealth games.

She longed to see Bhasker, being away for a long time; He too has risen far above her, but they were her sons; of that she was proud.
If only she could see him soon. She felt that she must.
  "Prem." She said, "Why don't we go to see Bhasker in his country." To her surprise, he was overwhelmed by eagerness too. "Sure, mum! We can use a holiday tour."

"Can you do it, Prem.? You have to undergo the training."

"Damn it! I want to see Bhasker too!"

"Then let us inform Bhasker."
Bhasker was overjoyed when his mother phoned "Mummy, are you coming. I will make all the arrangements. So long, mum, see you soon."

She knew he was stuck in a heavy routine of work that he enjoyed. She knew that her son would never utilize it for personal gain.
As they were seated in Air Scotland, she felt a thrill that her son was only five hours away within her reach. The thought filled her with happiness unsurpassed as yet. She looked at Prem, reclined in his seat sleeping unconsciously utterly

oblivious to the swaying of the giant air craft as it plowed its way through the gigantic clouds.

As Prem woke up, he saw his mother slightly dozing off; he looked at his watch; the radium plated numbers illuminated to show 17.45. The plane was about to land at Edinburgh within 15 minutes. The airhostess announced all passengers to fasten the seat belts and be ready for the landing.

Prem could see the giant Airliner swaying from side to side as the pilots braced for the landing. Happiness was reflected in Prem's mother's face; it would be a matter of minutes when she would see her son.

The sudden unexpected tragedy

But the next split second, hell broke loose, red alarm flashed in the airliner, the announcement sounded that a serious trouble has arisen, the plane was going for a crash-landing, passengers started screaming, and the shock and alarm exhibited in the passengers and airhostess were enough to confirm the disaster without a forewarning. Prem heard one of the passengers cry out "One of the back wheels is not working." He overheard the Airhostess' say "My God! The back wheel, one of them not budges out by the remote control."

Prem realized the gravity of the situation. What could the pilot do when a technical error occurs suddenly? It was too late to jerk the flight upwards as the signals, remote controls were alerted for the landing, the final thrust for the releasing of the back wheels was undertaken but unfortunately only one heavy tyre popped out, the other would not clear out, the airliner soared downwards at an astonishing speed, the pilot sweating at the controls.

Prem's mother started wailing, "My God! Why this!! Won't you allow me to see my son?"

Prem held her close to him, unmoved and indecisive of moment. "What could anyone do?" He thought.

Bhasker waiting at the Airport was shocked at the developments. The Airport was alerted for an emergency landing. Fire engines with sirens rushed to the landing zone, several ambulances were alerted and waited near the landing, Doctors and Nurses rushed outside the Airport to the runway with stretchers ready for the inevitable. Bhasker felt his body become numb. His mother and brother were inside and he could not fathom it in his mind any longer. He realized he had a duty to perform, he rushed to the area where the ambulance was parked ready, and the doctors were ready for any eventuality.

They saw the gigantic airliner advancing downwards like a giant hawk, suddenly landing with a thud on one back wheel, the other wheel scarcely out, a slight part of it was out rubbing violently on the runaway as the landing progressed on with a rushing speed; the friction from the rubbing on the runway could at any moment break apart the plane; but the front wheels landed in record time to balance the plane as it speeded along the runway. The sudden break applied caused a jerk and jolt among the passengers who faced the horror of the situation, completely paralyzed to face the worst. The plane zoomed along the runway, decreasing the speed as it went.

Fire engines with sirens ringing aloud raced along the runaway, followed by the ambulances.

The Airport Director was shouting orders, "Hurry! Take positions."

Before the plane grounded to a halt, flames started fuming from the cabins above the back wheels. The emergency exits were opened inside the plane; passengers terrified started rushing out madly by the staircase put up by the rescue teams. One by one, they were on a stampede inside injuring many women and children. Prem catching his mother's hand hurried through the exit; his mother was pulled out by the rescuers. Flames increased and gradually the cabins at the back were enveloped completely.

At any moment, the high speed jet engine oil may explode. Fire engines started spurting out large volumes of water from their hoses. Those who managed to come out were whisked away fast.

Bhasker saw his mother among those rescued, brought in.

He embraced his mother, "Mummy, where is Prem?"

"He is still there, helping those others to escape."

Bhasker could only admire the courage displayed by his brother. But his life was in danger. The plane may explode at any moment.

The next moment the massive airliner split in half as it exploded, smashing it from the middle to the tail.

Mother started screaming, Bhasker remained silent. As the fire engulfed the plane completely, some more passengers managed to escape. The Ambulance carried the seriously injured ones to the Multi-specialty Hospital near the Airport.

Bhasker had to go with them. As he looked at the scene of

the tragedy, all that was left of the plane was a huge roaring flame, red hot and fuming killing most of the passengers on board. It was a wonder that his mother escaped. But he had to see the seriously injured persons.

The doctors toiled tirelessly to save those who had been rescued. Most of the victims had first degree burns and succumbed to their injuries. Their bodies were laid on the Airport for their families to claim them.

Bhasker felt his knees sagging beneath him when the police uncovered the body of a young man under twenty. The face was charred beyond recognition disfigured, the youthful exuberance extirpated and all that remains were a gruesome figure.

Bhaskar recognizing the bracelet which his brother always more, on the wrist of the corpse, fell down beside it folding both his arms over his face, his mother hysterically shouted " my God , ! It was I who brought him to this!! Why didn't you take me too!! Bhaskar comforted her and said "Mother, I too feel the same. But strange are the ways of the Supreme, let us pray to Lord Krishna to receive his soul and bestow on him everlasting peace".

He felt a deep hollow uneasiness with in him, which had pieced his heart to torment him , his love for his brother was so intense that the grievous bodily harm within him upon the bereavement of his brother was in- calculable, incurable and inconsolable.
Indecision had kept him from contacting his Anna. Now he felt he needed a companion, to share the wound he felt deep within him; he had always loved Anna; Now out of a sudden impulse he remembered the phone number she had given as she had said to him, "My love, call me whenever you can. I

can never go on without you."

Remembering the happy times they had, he dialed the number; "Hello!" a soft voice answered "Hello! Can I speak to Anna?"

"Anna Fernandez, you mean," the women answered. "She is not here, left for New York with her husband a year ago."
    Hearing these words, he nearly dropped his phone "Hello! Hello! Who is it, please?"
    But he replaced the phone in the receiver.

"How stupid of me!" he thought.
    It was quite natural. He had not called her for a long, long time. His indecisive action has brought about this. She might have waited but for how long could a woman wait?

            Anyway he had lost her forever. His peace of mind was shattered beyond his control. He felt his mind was in turmoil. In such a pitiable condition, one would naturally resort to the inevitable, that of ending one's life on a sudden impulse. But as his mind was revolting with the idea, something noble in him kept him diverted from such a rash unmanly step. He felt that life was not to be as one would wish for but one's whole destiny is woven mysteriously by the Lord whom one can never understand here.

He felt that he was really made for the noble profession he was working. He had acquired an excellence in it and his fame extended far and wide in the world. He has still far to go before he retires from it.

One day his mother approached him and said "My son, you are advanced in years. It may not be long that I can be with you."

"What do you mean?" he enquired quietly.

"I hope you know what I mean," she said. "You should get married."

"No!" he replied. "I can never think of marriage now. I still have not got over the shock of losing my brother."

"My son, you will have to think of yourself. God has willed it this way."

"I have suffered greatly", she continued, "but it should be endured."

"But mother," he pleaded. "Please leave me alone."
Saying that he left her standing there musing while he went to his study-room.

Seeking a moment from the tension he felt.

There he was pondering over the happenings of the past till the present. The thought of his dear Anna filled his mind. He really missed her but he could never blame her for having married another. He had neglected her totally. She was devoid of his existence and had she known what he felt for her, she would never have taken the drastic step of choosing another partner. But now he felt foolish for the thought of her lovely face lighted up in his mind too late. But he knew he could never bring himself to think of another though she was lost forever. If only she had known what he felt for her even now?

His mind thus occupied, a sudden idea flashed to remove the uneasiness he felt within. The remembrance of the soiled map in his bag hidden for many years brought the expectation of a likely adventure which may bring a momentary relief from the present dejected situation. A momentary relief perhaps – but it would provide an encumbrance from the conflicting thoughts which seemed to have catapulted him to the extreme step of suicide.

He fished in his suitcase and after ransacking the contents, found the soiled paper. It was almost dilapidated and torn in several pieces. But after a tiring process, he managed to join them to disclose the message it conveyed.

The thought of the hidden treasures in the sea-depths did not invite the least interest to excite him but the adventure in seeking it. Though he was an expert swimmer and had learnt the art with Prem, he was nowhere close to him in prowess for his brother was stronger and swifter.

The preparedness for the journey was arranged with a captain of a yacht whom he knew. He listened patiently to what Bhasker had to say and made the arrangements to hire some trusted seafaring men and procure diving suits and weapons. Danger was imminent in the hidden depths and one has to be prepared in an eventuality.

Taking a long leave really shocked his colleagues but understanding his present dilemma, they readily complied by wishing him a happy vacation.

On the day the yacht was ready to sail, his mother came to see him off. She looked worn out, her eyes swollen from weeping and when she embraced him, she was shaking and clutching him wildly.

"My mother," he comforted her. "I won't be long away from you."

"But, my son," she said, "I have lost one and I cannot imagine another tragedy."

"Mother," he said, "you are aware that this holiday tour is just for a break – Do you prefer that my shattered mind break to pieces."
"No… No… my son," she said, "you are right".

"You will come back, my son, I need you, your profession and the world need you."

"Rest assured, mother," he replied.
He waved to his mother as the yacht slowly sailed away from the harbour. It was really majestic to see the big ships anchored at the wharf. The yacht swayed from side to side as the waves rose up and down by its side. The water looked pale green but later the color turned light blue. But as he looked further out to sea, it looked dark blue. The sea really fascinated him, he loved the waves, its splashing as it rose up to come down with a thunderous roar, then retreating backwards to come forward again sweep lashing everything in its way, never exhausted but ever presumptuous in its forward lashings which seemed to be strengthened at each tide. What he failed to realize – that the waves he marvels now can be a rogue when it arises as huge tidal waves wrecking destruction and havoc on human lives. Thousands had perished from the destruction wrought by tidal waves.

Such thoughts were non-existent and he was completely obsessed by the natural beauty of the sea, the play of the dolphins as they swam and tossed themselves high over the waters. Watching the dolphins, he felt a surge of joy within at the thought of joining them to partake in their pleasurable company.

After hours of sailing over the calm ocean, the captain signaled to him that they had finally arrived at the site – as indicated in the map. The compass and other nautical instruments confirmed it.

Putting on the diving suits, he boldly ventured to explore the depths with the aid of two other divers. They accompanied him down with weapons in their hands. They swam below, diving deeper and deeper. A world of nature's wonder exhibited in their entire splendor far below the depths. Colourful fishes of all sizes moved among the shoal of fishes circling around the water. At times they kept a distance as huge sharks swam to feed on them. These carnivores would not hesitate to attack humans.

It was then that they saw it – a huge dark object sunk far below. As they neared it, the remnants of an old wrecked ship were visible. Gradually they inched their way closer, finally they bounded it, but the ship was damaged beyond recognition – a space of several long years in the depth might have brought about this – major parts having been washed away.

They searched inside for what they had come for but their efforts seemed futile. After several hours they abandoned the ship and swam back to the yacht. Exhausted, Bhasker might have slept for a long time for when he awoke, it was past midnight. Not one of the men or the captain was seen. He got up and walked on the deck unmindful of everything except the silence of the night. The yacht was anchored in the mid-ocean, unmoving and everything appeared to be dead and silent like the Tale of the Ancient Mariner.

Suddenly a hand rested on his shoulder. He turned around wildly to confront the captain.

"Oh! Is it you," Bhasker asked, "You really shocked me."

"I saw you absorbed in the silence of the night," the captain said.

"What are your plans?" Bhasker asked.

"Should we continue our search?"

"Yes, I think so! Just one more try. Just to make sure. Then we will be on our way," Bhasker said.

When they plunged into the depths for a last attempt, they were stupefied at the sight of a monstrous gigantic mass of flesh moving along the side of the wreck. The enormous hulk of a whale, which if provoked, could be dangerous, for it could break a ship into pieces by smashing it but he knew that in spite of its huge size, it was extremely harmless. It drifted to one side as they neared. Getting bolder, he attempted to touch and caress it, feeling the coarse skin of the greatest mammal that ever lives now. After an intensive search, the idea that the treasure might have been lost or taken was clearly intelligible. They decided to rescind their project and return home. The trip was not without its reward for the serenity of his mind could not have been attained if he had stayed at home.

A REMARKABLE COINCIDENCE

Immediately on his arrival, Bhasker was summoned by the Ministry of Health to attend the conference of world Heart

153

Specialists at Paris.

His passport and visa had been processed and he arrived at the Airport to board the Air France flight to France. As he cleared the customs, he noticed a peculiar resemblance in one of the Air hostesses walking briskly past to board the flight. Immediately, he recognized the lady to be none other than Anna. He could not visualize how Anna appeared so suddenly and before he could call out, she had passed him on her way to the plane. His heart was thumping madly as he could not imagine that after all these years, he had glimpsed her visage for a fleeting second. He knew he was boarding the same flight; so the thought of seeing her excited him beyond his imagination.

One by one the passengers started boarding the flight as the announcement was made. As Bhasker boarded the plane, two Air hostesses were at the entrance passage-way greeting the passengers. Anna was clearly seen standing at the doorway. As he neared her to enter inside, he greeted her, "Good morning, Anna, how are you, my dear." A change came over Anna as if she had an electric shock. Her eyes widened and her lips and mouth parted and she blurted out, "Good morning," then almost immediately added, "My God, Bhasker, you….. " He patted her on the shoulder, "Anna, come and see me when you are free." He walked briskly to his seat leaving her staring at him as if she had seen a ghost. After having seated himself, he looked in her direction. She was still gazing at him with wonder and a smile was displayed on her face.

All the passengers fastened their seat belts and the massive plane took off with a thunderous roar into the sky, rising higher and higher. Finally the flight being air-borne, the air hostesses and stewards started issuing refreshments.

It was then that she came over to him. "Bhasker," she smiled, "you really surprised me after all these years."
"I am also equally shocked, my dear," he exclaimed.

"We shall meet in the Hotel."

He gave her a card and the Hotel No.
"Where are you off to," she asked.

"I have to attend a conference tomorrow at Paris, he replied.

"Anna," he continued. "We have to talk in private. I will expect you."

"Sure," she said while she resumed her duty.

After the plane had landed at Paris, he was whisked off by an arranged taxi to a five-star hotel. The hotel was marvelous and well-furnished to suit the tastes of the most elite class. After a refreshing bath, he might have dozed for some time when the sound of a bell awoke him.

When he opened the door, the sight of his Anna standing there was enough to re-awaken the love he had for Anna ever since they had met.
"Hello, Bhasker, how are you," she said.

Anna looked so wondrously fair and slim, her eyes so piercingly fixed on him, her lip so voluptuously red, her skirt neatly stitched to expose her perfectly shaped thighs and legs in her uniform.

"Hello, Anna, please come in," he said softly.

When she was seated, he managed to continue, "Anna, when

155

did you join Air France."

"Two years back" she replied.

"Where is your husband?" he asked suddenly.

She got up started. "How did you know?" she enquired.

"I phoned your house two years back. You had gone to America with him, I was told," Bhasker replied.

"Yes, but I was not happy with him. I divorced him and returned. He was a rogue and cared not for me," she said.

"Was it so serious that you had to take such a drastic step?"

"It all started on the very first night I told him I loved another," she said.

"Why?" Bhasker asked.

"I still madly love you." She replied.

"Then why did you marry him?"

"My parents forced me," she replied, "and I didn't know where you were."

"Where is your wife?" she asked suddenly.

"Do you mean my wife … what?" Bhasker stammered. "Do you think I would marry when I have always loved… you?"

"What!! Do you really mean it?" she asked, "you are …. Not married … till now."

"No, my dear," he replied. "I could not think of another woman. I phoned you once .... But you had left with another--forever.

"My dear... dear Bhasker," she repeated. "Do you still love me?"
Slowly he edged towards her, "My life would never be complete without you, my Anna."

She embraced Bhasker and held on tight to him. Then she pulled his face to her and kissed him passionately on the lips.

But he pushed her back saying, "Will you... Anna ... marry me?

"Marry you," cried Anna "My dear, I am yours forever."
She clung to him and him to her. They knew that they were not to be separated for ever... ever.
Anna re-awakened in him a sexual desire which had been dormant for a long, long time. He remembered a prostitute who had tried to seduce him but failed. However, she tried, he could not be roused.

Finally she had said, "You will be a failure in sexual intercourse."

Utterly dejected, he had avoided women believing he could be impotent. But at times, he dreamt he was kissed by girls Now it was different. Anna kindled in him a desire which he had not known before. A mere touch of the softness of her body was enough giving a pleasure he had not known before.

Bhasker's mind was preoccupied with thoughts of their future. He was of the firm belief that he had dishonored her by not marrying her at once. He felt that he should not delay it further.

"Anna", Bhasker said suddenly embracing her, "why don't we get married right away."

"Do you really want to," asked Anna looking thoughtfully at him.

"Want to, definitely, since you are my wife now."
"Do you love me, Bhasker," she asked.

"My darling!" he replied as he embraced her kissing her on her lips which were parted.

"My dear," she said suddenly, "What if I could not conceive and give you a child."

"That will not bother me as I am more concerned in having you as a companion for life," said Bhasker.

"But don't you want to have a child," remarked Anna.

"Anna, let us not talk about such things now," he said.

"What I really want is ... You and you only for the rest of my life." he added.

"Bhasker, I too love you so much, darling!"

"Then let us get married in a registrar office to get it sanctified."
Two days later they were married with only a few close friends of Bhasker to bear witness to the remarkable event. Bhasker had insisted on the marriage not to be publicized.

"I would have been happier if my mother were here," said Bhasker to Anna.

"Why is she not here," she enquired.

"I didn't tell her about you"

"Why?"

"She may not approve of you. You belong to a different nationality."

"But you should have told her, my dear."

"Sure, but it will take time for mother to adjust to you."

"Let us forget everything else. I am about to give you a surprise."

An Emergency .

"What is that?"

We are just about to travel on a pleasure trip for two weeks to Switzerland."

"How wonderful!!" she was overjoyed and said, "Is it for our honeymoon?

"Yes, don't you approve it?"

"Really! You're wonderful!" she exclaimed embracing him.

159

The next two days Anna busied herself in packing the necessary items needed for the journey. On the night before the reckoning date of the journey, she was discussing what they could do during the trip.

"How exhilarating!! We could climb the mountains, ski, and go boating and so many fun-related events.

"Sure, my dear, we can do all that but the important thing is that you are with me," said Bhasker.

The ringing of the telephone in the next room brought him to his senses. Excusing himself, he walked briskly out. Anna fancied herself already in Switzerland, completely absorbed in her dreams that she did not notice Bhasker had returned.

"My dear Anna," said Bhasker

"Something has happened."

"What is it, my dear?"

"I have to cancel my pleasure trip. But you can proceed to Switzerland."
"What do you mean?" said Anna

"I have been called to Delhi to operate on a heart's transplant for the richest tycoon in India."

"Then cancel the trip to Switzerland and I want to be with you. Don't leave me here."

"If you wish to come with me, you are welcome."

"Wherever you go, I will be with you."

160

They had their flight tickets Okayed. Soon they were on the plane flying to Delhi.

"Anna, I am really sorry, "said Bhasker.

"You don't have to, your duty comes first. I am really happy to be with you."

On landing at Delhi International Airport, Doctor Bhasker and Anna were accorded a warm welcome by a uniformed chauffeur who escorted them to a Mercedes Benz car parked nearby. They were driven to the Jaslok Hospital. A group of doctors awaited their arrival. Bhasker was garlanded and taken to the Director's room.

The Director's room was well spacious decorated with rich costly furniture's and all the modern facilities available in a V.I.P's room.
As they entered, the Director stood up to receive Bhasker. He appeared to be a man of immense size, broad at the shoulders and standing well above six feet.

"Dear, dear Bhasker, so you have come. Now that you are here, we are doubly sure of success."

Before Bhasker could reply, he exclaimed, "Hello! Who is this? Your wife."

"Yes, Sir," Bhasker replied.

"How do you do", said the Director.

"Anna, Anna Bhasker," she calmly replied.
"Congratulations, Bhasker, but you never invited us at all."

161

"Sir, it was not publicized."

"Excuse me, Anna, can I talk with your husband for some time."

She nodded. The Director led Bhasker inside and related the circumstances that led to the urgency in calling him at once. He related that the man in question was the richest businessman in India. His name was Sanjeev Reddy. The Prime Minister had specifically mentioned that the best heart transplant surgeon should be made available for the surgery.

"So, Bhasker, you know the facts. It will depend on your expertise. The man's life must be saved. I was told the condition is extremely critical."

"Could I see the report of the physical check-ups?"

"One thing more, Bhasker, concentrate on your wisdom alone as you are extraordinary in every way."
"Sir, I don't need persuasion to do my duty. For me all patients are alike. I do not consider them different."

"That's true, but Bhasker!! The country needs this man."

"I will do what I can. The rest is in the hands of the unseen power."

"Now if you don't mind, the patient has requested your presence with your wife to meet him."

They were escorted to a large air – conditioned room. Five guards with machine guns were posted at the door. On seeing them they lowered their guns and saluted. Bhasker returned the salute. On entering, they saw a bed with the most modern amenities. Two guards were posted on either side of the bed. A man richly clothed but frail in appearance lay on the bed. He appeared to be near the seventies.

On seeing them enter the room, he tried to move but Bhasker quickly moved closer to the patient and said softly "Sir, don't worry, I have come. All will be well." Sanjeev made an effort to speak, 'Thank you, Doctor, I am hopeful now. Save me and you will get half of my wealth." Anna gasped when she heard this. But Bhasker replied "No, dear sir, I don't require wealth. I will do my best."

"That . . . . is . . . . enough, doctor. I . . . . . . am . . . hopeful. .. . . .Thank you." whispered Sanjeev.

"Good day, Sir," said Bhasker and left the room with Anna.

"Bhasker, it is really pitiful, the state of the patient is critical," said Anna.

"I know, my dear, but I will try"... Anna could easily perceive that all the doctors in this well known Hospital regarded Bhasker with renown and as a person with God-given powers to heal and cure in the realm of medicine. He never talks about his profession and so she had no idea that her husband was regarded as the most famous surgeon in heart-transplant in India.

On the night before the fixed day of the famous surgery, Bhasker was extremely without any signs of tension, but relaxed in mind and body. When she turned to him, he engulfed her in his arms, kissing her in the mouth while slowly moving his hands over her thighs and buttocks. She tried to pull away saying, "My dear, don't overexert yourself.

Tomorrow is the day." But Bhasker pulled her closely and said, "Don't worry, I need this now. You are my strength now."

As he entered her, she cried out, "Dear Bhasker, I never imagined such a power in you."

"That is what I saved for you alone as I have had no other lovers."

Soon it was consummated by both of them coming to a climax at the same time.

The Open heart Surgery

The next day when Anna awoke, she was surprised to find Bhasker had gone.
She saw a note beside her "sorry, darling. Sleep well. I will be back later."
She knew that breakfast would be provided at the hospital. She was worried about the outcome of the operation. But the extraordinary prowess and expertise of her husband in surgery is indubitable.

At the hospital, the surgery for the heart-transplant was conducted in a graceful manner by a team of doctors headed by Dr.Bhasker. These doctors were highly specialized and skilled in having performed many heart-transplants before successfully. But even minute errors could complicate the process. Hence, these doctors who were performing the surgery were selected from a team of doctors who were infallible in their past and present achievements.
Dr.Bhasker was epitomizing the dexterity of his nimble fingers as he worked timelessly on. Twelve long hours he toiled with the others. The whole process of removing the

164

sickly damaged heart and replacing it with a donor's heart needed a perfection which could only be achieved by a highly competent surgeon.

News had flashed all over Delhi. Newspaper reporters, photographers, video graphers were at close quarters. Outside the surgery room, a crowd had gathered behind to wait as eye-witnesses.

Anna was wonderstruck at the pandemonium occurring which would have worsened had it not been for the guards and police assembled to curb these people to remain passive.

Finally after three more long hours, the surgery room opened. Dr.Bhasker was the first one out followed by the other doctors.

"The surgery is over. It has been a remarkable success," he said. Immediately there was uproar from the crowd." "Congratulations, Dr.Bhasker."

"Long live Dr.Bhasker."

Reporters and video- graphers started questioning and flashing video cameras. Anna looked at Dr.Bhasker as he was escorted out by the guards and policemen.

Suddenly he saw her and he raised his hand. She too raised hers and smiled. Well done!! My dear," she shouted. He came straight towards her and held her to him. Photographers started flashing photos of them. He felt exhausted and they were taken in princely style in the most expensive car ever seen to their home.

When they were finally alone, he said, "I feel so tired, darling.

Could you give me coffee and snacks?"

"You deserve more than that, my dear. Wait a minute; I will make it in a minute."

The incessant ringing of the phone at regular intervals caused a lot of inconvenience to Dr. Bhasker even though they were full of praises to him which he deserved as he was not at all ostentatious.

The Invitation.

Three months later Bhasker received a call from the business Magnate Mr.Sanjeev Reddy, inviting him to be present with his wife at a grand function in his house. Important dignitaries were invited and Sanjeev insisted on his presence there. Before Bhasker could intervene to decline the offer, the phone was cut off after Mr.Sanjeev had added that he would be sending his personal chauffeur and car to fetch him.

At exactly eight O'clock in the night the chauffeur came and Bhasker and Anna were taken to the party. Bhasker was dressed in a blue suit and pants with a matching blue tie, Anna wore a pink sparkling type of blouse and skirt which reached far below her knees. She looked so stunningly beautiful and fair that any onlookers would care to gaze at her. Looking at her striding across the room, one would be transported to the world of fantasy where she would appear as a fairy queen of the wonderland.

As they were escorted by two guards to the room after reaching there, many continued to glance in her direction marveling at her body shape and figure. Anna seemed to be

166

unmindful of the attention she was gaining from the male onlookers. Mr.Sanjeev Reddy was waiting for them.

"Welcome! Dr.Bhasker & Mrs.Bhasker. We are fortunate that you have come."

He embraced Mr.Bhasker and smiled at Anna. He introduced them to the Prime Minister and his wife. The P.M. was about Mr.Bhasker's stature, somewhat close to six feet two, wide at the shoulders and stout in stature. The Prime-minister's wife was below the average height of a woman, slender and dressed in a grey sari. But her age may be somewhere near the middle of forties. When compared with her husband, she appeared too short. Yet it was seen that they were perfectly at ease with each other.

"Hello! Mr.Bhasker," said the P.M. "I am pleased to meet you, doctor. As a practitioner, you have come a long way, I am sure you will go a long way further." "Thank you, Sir; I am honored to meet you."
"Mr.Bhasker, I have been persuaded by Mr.Sanjeev to divulge something which you would not acquiesce." said the P.M.

"So he has got it sanctified through a court of law to bequeath a property consisting of a bungalow to you with all rights conferred on you. Here is the will bearing his signature and the witnesses' signatures. He has entreated me to make you to accept it as a token of gift."

So saying the P.M. handed to Mr.Bhasker the will. Bhasker was hesitating when Anna overhearing all, stepped forward and said," Bhasker, dear, accept it as it is given as a gift."

Anna pressed Mr.Bhasker's hand and re-assured him.

He accepted the will, "please tell Mr.Sanjeev that I do accept it not as a token of payment but as a mode of friendship, I accept it as he has given it in good faith."

CHAPTER 8 A STRANGE HAPPENING NOTICED

Anna noticed a sudden change in Bhasker as he returned from the Hospital one day. He was incommunicative as to the course of events which had caused it. At first his moody behavior was inconspicuous but to Anna who knew Bhasker immensely, the real cause for it was not perceptible to her even.

"Tell me, Bhasker, what is troubling you," Anna asked him.

"Nothing... Nothing... why?" he enquired.

"Don't try to misguide me, I know you only too well,"

"But I don't think you would believe it once told. He said.

"Now, please tell me."

"Anna, it is about a boy who is at the hospital now." He said.
"What about him?"

"The incident he related to me shocked me beyond my senses."

169

"Dear Bhasker, don't try to play riddles, get to the facts."

"All right," said Bhasker.

"Have I told you about my brother who was badly burnt to death while rescuing passengers from a plane crash-landed ten years ago?"

"Yes, you have. Your younger brother, Prem. Isn't it?"

"What has that to do with this, dear," Anna enquired.
"A lot, Anna," said Bhasker emotionally agitated. "I asked him to tell me about him. Then he said he remembered his past life of how he had saved passengers on a burning plane, how his mother escaped, how he was badly burnt when he had blacked out."

"Did he relate anything else," asked Anna.
"No, he remembers only this incident. He even remembers his name as Prem in his past life. He told me that he occasionally have hallucinations which rouses him from sleep."

"What would be his age now?"

"Ten years as seen in the medical report."

"Do you believe he is telling the truth?"

"How could he, a small boy, guess it? Only I know the incident. Besides the only other person who knows it is my mother."
"Do you then believe that the boy could be ..?" Anna asked.
"May be, guessing the age, it could be possible. Life's mystery is truly mysterious."

"Nobody would believe in it," Anna remarked.

"Dear Anna, when factual truth is substantiated by evidence, it has to be believed. It is rather strange that there are more mysteries in the universe than we can dream of."

"What about his parents. Are they with him?" she enquired.

"I have talked with them. They feel that their child may be affected by brain fever as he continuously raves and shouts in sleep."

"The only possibility for a recovery to a normal state is to give counseling to the boy that dreams and hallucinations are not real but conflicting emotions of the mind. The child had been advised not to take a realistic approach to the fancies or imagination passing through the mind. Human mind is complex which may keep wandering if we are unable to restrain it."

"Now that you know," said Anna. "Don't you want to intimate that you were his brother?"

"No, Anna," he said, "That would intimidate matters worse. The real truth about life is always hidden. Let it remain so."

Bhasker's anxiety.

As the months passed, Anna was surprised at the attachment of her husband towards her increasing at an alarming pace. She knew that he loved her beyond measure. One day Bhasker was surprised to find that Anna was not at home when he returned. He waited impatiently. He could not bear even a moment without her.

Suddenly Anna appeared carrying a basket of fruits and vegetables.

"Anna, where were you?" shouted Backer.

"Went to the market, dear," said Anna.

"There was no need for that," he said. "You could have phoned me."

"What is the matter?"

"I don't want you to go out."
"But why, dear, I am bored sitting at home."

"Oh now you are bored already," said Bhasker.

"Why do you say that?"

"I want you always with me when I am around."

"But it was only for a moment."

"No matter, Anna, I want you to be always at home."

Seeing him so hot-tempered for such a flimsy reason, she could not
Help laughing. Bhasker too felt a sudden impulse to join in, but embraced her.

"My dear Irish lady, I love you so much."

172

"I too, love you, Dear Bhaskar".

"Don't you see", said Anna, "It is almost time for someone else to be with us. That would make our life worth living for,"

"Don't you realize what I mean?" she continued.

"Do you mean my Mum? She's coming tomorrow, my dear."

Oh! That's not what I meant, dear." Anna replied, "I'm happy she's coming but don't you realize that we should have a baby."

"Yes, said Bhasker, "Do you feel so?"

Bhasker held her closer to him and started kissing her saying,

"Anna, definitely you shall have a baby. Meanwhile let me tell you good news. My mum is arriving next week. She phoned me when I was at the Hospital and she's dying to meet you."

"Oh! My Bhasker! I'll be so happy to see her but will she accept me as her daughter."

"My Anna! You don't really know her. She would love you as she loves me. She has no one else other than us.

The arrival of Bhasker's Mum.

On the day Bhasker's Mum, Smitha arrived at the international Indira Gandhi Airport; both Bhasker and Anna

173

were at the airport to receive her. Bhasker was dressed in a plain white shirt and he wore white jeans, his mother's favorite color as he believed. He looked so dashingly handsome, his hair cut short to make him look still younger than he was. Moreover she had not seen him for years. Anna was dressed in tight fitting jeans and a shirt concealing the upper portion of her body to a satisfactory portion so as not to displease her incoming mother-in-law who has not seen her yet. She looked so pretty that onlookers were staring at her that it annoyed Bhasker.

As the Plane landed, they waited for a moment. Within minutes, the passengers were seen briskly walking out through the customs. The passengers were too many and Bhasker was not able to trace his Mum among the crowd of ladies, children, and gents as there were many elderly people coming out at that moment.

Then he saw his mother coming out of the exit door. She had grown fairly old and she looked tired and exhausted. She wore a beautiful orange colored sari for that was her best selection, Bhasker remembered ten years before. Then he realized that ten years have dragged by since he had seen his mother. How could she have passed her time all alone by herself? Although she has completed forty-five years of age, she walked with a steady pace. When she noticed him, she immediately smiled and rushed over to his side. They embraced each other and she was crying in joy for they had been away from each other for ten long years. Bhasker had not lived apart from his mother this long and he regretted it now. He remembered that when he was young he used to follow her everywhere. They used to gossip away the full day long, listening to her stories of old. She had always been a source of inspiration to him in times of difficulties.

She looked by her side and recognized immediately the

174

beautiful lady standing close to them. She smiled as she saw her daughter-in- law stepping forward.

Smitha gripped Anna firmly with both her hands and said, "Dear, how pretty you are? So you were the one I hadn't seen but I was kept guessing... How happy I'm to see you now, my dear girl. He has told me all. I'm not all surprised."

Oh! Mum, I'm so thrilled..." Anna replied.

" My Dear, I told him I wanted to see you but my son Bhasker felt it was not the time for us to meet then. " Smitha said.

"You mean you were not opposed to our relationship." Anna said.

"Never, my dear," Smitha said, "true love can never be shattered by anyone."

"I'm truly glad to know that you think so," said Anna.

Bhasker was looking on with a smile on his lips. He was happy that his mother had accepted her without even a slight objection.

"Mama," he said, "You understand me better than I do".

"Dear children", said Smitha, "ten years had passed since you married, yet you don't have a baby"

Both Bhasker & Smitha were embarrassed when they heard this.

"Mummy," said Bhasker, "we don't want it so soon, you know, we want to enjoy life and later think about it"

"What do you mean, my son", a baby is important in a

married life. There are many who don't have children when
they want them so much."
 Suddenly she felt embarrassed in front of her daughter-in-
law and she said,
"Ok, let's not talk about it, Smitha said, "If you feel like it."

Their ride in Bhasker's car brought Smitha to admire him, as
he drove through the busy highway with a skill she was
unaware of. After fifteen minutes drive, they stopped before
a mansion that looked almost like a palace to her. Her son
should be immensely rich to own such a house with a wide
courtyard and drive-in, that was normally in the possession
of very wealthy people. True, this spacious mansion was
given to Bhasker as a gift by a wealthy man whom Bhasker
had saved years back. Bhasker had brought him back to life
through a heart surgery.

There was a swimming pool inside that attracted the
attention of Smitha. The pool was large, rectangular in shape
and beside the pool; many sliding chairs placed near for the
convenience of lying in a sleeping position. Colourful
umbrellas spread out were fixed on the ground to give shade
for shielding against the extreme heat of the sun at noon.
The water in the pool seemed to sparkle like diamonds when
the sun rays were reflected in it. Smitha felt enchanted to be
in such a beautiful place.

When she stepped into the house, she was indeed astonished
as it resembled the spacious floorings of exquisite marbles
that was similar to Taj Mahal, one of the grand wonders of
the world. There were rooms in plenty and she wondered
that there were enough rooms to accommodate people to
live in it as a five-star hotel. The internal furnishings and
furniture were all imported from other countries and the
rooms were all decorated with rich carpets spread out in

every room. Smitha felt that the grandeur of the ancient Mughal Emperor's palace was seen all over the place. She felt so happy for her son and Anna too, came far above her expectations.

That evening his Mum retired for the night. From the window she could see the evening sun had slowly changed to a lovely red ball, sinking slowly down in the far distant sky. She admired the glory of sunset that had brightened the sky to a dazzling color, far beyond in comparison to other marvels of nature that she had witnessed.

For a moment, her thoughts flashed back to the past. She saw her younger son engulfed in flames and he had lost his life in saving others in the burning plane. Before he died in the flames of first degree burns, he had saved his Mum from the disaster. She could not control her tears when she remembered the incident. Eleven years before, the tragedy had occurred but the memory of her son was clear in her memory. She could see a faint glimpse of her son, dead eleven years ago, looking down at her from among the clouds. The shadow of his physical form was visible to her as the clouds were changing color and moving hastily towards its destination. Tears started rolling down her eyes and a mist shadow covered her eyes, blocking out everything out of her sight.

Soon darkness enveloped the place but the mansion where she lay was lighted up with brightness from different types of neon lamps. The whole mansion appeared as a fairy land where a magical charm seemed to be prevalent round the place.
In her restless state of mind, she got off the bed and walked downstairs. Her son and Anna were surprised to see her as they thought that she might have dozed off.

177

"Mum! Aren't you sleepy? We thought you might have slept by now." said Bhasker.

"I couldn't as I was thinking of Prem", said Smitha.

"Are you still troubled by his memory?" asked Bhasker.

"I can never forget him," said Smitha.

"Thinking of him wouldn't help us any more, you know, Mum," he said.

'I'm sorry to remind you of him to disturb your piece of mind" .she said.

"Not at all, Mum! We can't buck off fate that controls us. Some of us die young and it's said that good souls leave early. Rest assured he had found eternal peace that we'd never find here.
Let's try to forget the past, Mum. Good night!"

"Good night!" reciprocated Smitha to her son.

As Bhasker lay beside his wife Anna, she turned to him and enquired," What's wrong? Is your Mum restless after the day's journey?"

"Yeah, something worse than that seems to trouble her".

"What may be that?"

"Nothing really serious but her mind is still preoccupied with the thoughts of my younger brother who had died many years ago."

"Maybe she feels she has been neglected for so long," she remarked," but she don't have to as she's with us."

Bhasker was awakened from a sound sleep by a loud scream which was heard from the room where his mother slept. He got up hurriedly, almost jumping from the bed and rushed to the place, followed by Anna close by his side.

They saw Smitha in an excited state of mind and when she saw them, she hysterically called out, "Bhasker! I saw him right in front me, gazing at me".

"Who do you mean? There's no one else inside the house other than us," said Bhasker.

Smitha said slowly, uttering the words in a slow motion, "Yes, I saw my son, Prem looking at me in the darkness and he wanted to talk with me."

"Mum! Bhasker retorted, "This's ridiculous! You are imagining things."

"No!" she shouted annoyingly," I saw him as I see you right now. Moreover I was wide awake. He looked exactly the same as I knew him. The only difference being that his eyes looked as if they were bloodthirsty and out of place from the real Prem who I had known as my child."

Bhasker and Anna looked at each other in disbelief mingled with a sense of horror. Something awakened their senses to realize that there may be a shade of truth in Smitha's outburst.

"Mum! Could you tell us in detail about the apparition that you saw?"

You still think I'm not telling the truth. But I tell you plainly I saw him coming towards me. I wasn't afraid as I thought I was seeing my long lost son. But the piercing gaze of his bloodthirsty eyes frightened me to call out. The eyes don't seem to fit my son whom I knew. When I called out, he disappeared as he had come."

"But, Mum! We have been here for many years and nothing like this has occurred", said Bhasker.

"Unbelievable! And totally incredulous," said Anna.

"My dear Anna! You too will change your opinion when you see what I have seen," said Smitha.

"O.K. Mum! We will sleep here by your side this night."
"No! No! You needn't as I 'm not afraid to be alone. Besides what I have seen is the apparition of my son."

"O.K. mum. If you feel that that." said Bhasker and left the room with Anna.

Next day, Bhasker awoke as the light flickering rays of the sun was seen emanating through the window screens in his room. He got up hurriedly and went outside to his garden to inhale the pure air in the morning breeze. As usual, he concentrated on his yoga exercises for more than thirty minutes. Utterly oblivious of everything else, his mind was lost in the sensuous beauty of nature that he enjoyed so much. Even then, he could faintly hear the chirping of birds and the chattering of monkeys that swung from the trees close to his home. Nearby lay a forest clearing, thickly populated on either side by a thickset of foliage of trees. The height of the trees towered like giants that stood rooted to hide the glorious sunshine. The trees spread out like a dark blanket around the surrounding area for miles around that the daylight seemed hardly visible at the place where Bhasker's home lay.

Bhasker, during his childhood days, had always wondered what it would be like to live in an isolated place. He specially loved the sights of the forest where he could enjoy and feel the beauty of nature and its denizens as they roamed the place. It was a customary habit of his to lie on his reclining seat in the balcony to enjoy the coolness and solitude of the forest area. He used to spend hours of his time lost in thoughts of his own. At these moments, Anna hardly disturbed him.

Now that his mother was with him, he was happy and wanted to please her in every way. She had been away from him for a long while and he felt he owed everything to her for his success in life.

Two months passed and Smitha felt it was time for her to leave. Bhasker was overwhelmed with grief when he realized that his Mum had decided to go back to her hometown. The land of Kerala had a nostalgic effect on her and her son knew that once her mind was made up, nothing could force her to change it.

"My son, I have to go back to my place", she said.

"What do you mean by that? Bhasker asked perplexed by her decision, "Are you not pleased to be here with me."

"No, my son," she said," It is not because I'm not happy here but I can get peace of mind when I 'm alone. I don't want to you to be so agitated thinking about me. I can take care of myself and I'm better off alone.

"Mum!" he said, "I 'm now so happy you had come to me and never thought you'd go back."

"My dear! Don't you realize that we all have to depart at one time and that could be at any moment." she said, "The sooner the better. Enjoy your moments with your wife. I want to retire to a life of solitude, meditate and know the truth about life. A new adventure I seek different from what I have known before. I feel the only way to realize the ultimate truth is to detach myself from all the materialistic issues. Thoughts and desires have to be cast aside. I'm going to withdraw from the mainstream society and be a yogi to learn something more."

"Are you crazy, Mum?" Bhasker enquired.

"No! I have been haunted by such thoughts ever since childhood. In the ancient times, Buddha had abandoned his princely status, his wife and his family to seek enlightenment. He succeeded in finding the truth about existence. I mean to follow the same path. The truth if revealed to me by meditation could relieve me from my deep attachment for my dead son."

Bhasker found it difficult to reply as the truth that his mother sought was beyond his intelligence. He knew that his thoroughly educated Mum was well aware of what she was saying.

Bhasker's new revelation.

The sudden decision of his Mum to seek a path of revelation to the Truths that had been hidden from all, even now, seem bleak for years and years to come. Bhasker was fully conscious that the human mind was incapable of ascending the elusive immeasurable heights of knowledge, to learn the actual Truth that mystifies us all. Then how could his Mum succeed in ascending such misty dizzy heights. Such thoughts had been racing in his mind since he had been a child. Bhasker was under the delusion that the answer to all these conflicting thoughts could well be a big zero. Nevertheless he was of the view that there has to be a solution and a meaning to the wonderful aspects of nature that surrounds us amidst its mysticism.

The thoughts that his Mum was about to leave him to an abode of loneliness that she preferred would bring a change in her, was unintelligible as he could surmise. He knew he has to persuade her to abandon her resolution to part with him forever, for as far as he was aware, it was a foolish venture that she had decided. It was not for us humans to track down the unfamiliar path that would lead us nowhere to the Truth, hidden in the depth of which, we humans can never fathom.

He felt that he had to sway her mind somehow to make her change her mind. Then it dawned on him that there was one thing that had been harboring within him for a long time, causing doubts and uncertainty. It was about the boy that he had come to know some years back. That boy, merely ten years old, had mysteriously revealed his past as he had said in an incident pointing to Bhasker's brother Prem and Mum in a plane crash. Bhasker felt that now he had to reveal it to Mum, otherwise he may never get the chance.

"Mum"! He said excitedly," You ought to know something. I kept it away from you as I felt it was bull-shit. But now I feel that there's something in it. Mum! I hope you don't think I'm crazy but I saw the boy and he told me about the plane crash in which you and Prem met the tragic mishap."

"Well1 What about it and what did the boy tell you", asked Bhasker's Mum.

"You ought to be surprised to know that he related the whole incident as he had been involved in it as an active person. The shocking fact in his outburst was that he was Prem who had met the tragic death in a previous birth. He even mentioned that his mother was with him at that time. His parents thought their son was raving owing to hallucinations.

"My goodness! cried out Mum," But didn't you ask him any more of what he knew."

'No! Mum! I was stumped and I felt weak then. I could not speak out anything. Neither could I bring myself to ask him further anything in case of embarrassing his parents who were present with him in the hospital."

Mum was too exhilarated that she burst out saying," Take me to him immediately. I want to see him to learn more than what anyone could offer to enlighten me on the mystery of reincarnation."

"But, Mum! Do you feel there is any truth in thinking so?"
"Why not," she said," What else you want as proof when you are aware that he has related the tragic scene that had occurred many years ago affecting us all."

"Where is that boy now? Take me to him if he is nearby."

"No! Mum, he lives with his parents in the outskirts of Punjab and if you wish I'll take you to him." said Bhasker.

The very next day in the early hours of daybreak, when the sun had risen and the flashes of the sunlight rays had brightened the world that consisted of Bhasker's home; He, Anna and his Mum, set out on a quest to inquire as they believed, a highly preposterous truth, given out by a child. Mum was too excited, as Bhasker could make out, thinking by herself and deeply contemplative. No one spoke anything during the trip as they didn't know what to expect from a mere child of ten years of age.

After hours of driving, Bhasker turned back in his car to see that both his Mum and Anna were exhausted. They were reclining in their seats, lost in the world of dreams while he, conscious of the fact that he was driving, had to be alert and awake. Suddenly Anna awoke and looking outside through the side glass, saw the beauty of the landscape outside. On both sides of the road, she glimpsed the wheat grains and corns in golden color flaying and dancing in the breeze that beat about them. The site was amazing for anyone who sees it for the first time. They had entered the rich expanse of land of the countryside of Punjab.

"What a beauty"! It looks like a wonderland, numerous corns lie stretching for miles around in the landscape," she remarked.

Bhasker's Mum too awoke and was wonderstruck at the heavenly sight that enfolded before them.
"This's indeed a heavenly sight. Are we really in heaven to see wonderful scenery and hear amazing things." said Mum who was wide awake now.

"If you think so, Mum, This is a heaven for some people,"

185

said Bhasker.

"Have we neared the place?" asked Mum eagerly.
"Almost nearing," said Bhasker, as he drove on uninterrupted by the conversation which ensued forth.

"There're very few people around and hardly any dwellings seen for miles in this place," said Mum.

"This is the food provider zone for the entire country and millions in India escape starvation from the produces from this rich agricultural land." said Bhasker.

"Look there!" said Bhasker to his Mum and Anna, "Can't you see a speck in the distance?

"Where?" asked Anna for they could not see more than a tiny spot?"
As the car sped on, Bhasker said, "There in the distance you can view a tiny hut. There're no others huts nearby." We are going to that hut as the object of our search is residing in that hut."

"What!" enquired both Anna and his Mum? "You mean that the boy lives there".
"Yeah, his parents tills and supervises the land for the land owner of this area," said Bhasker.
When he reached the place, there was a narrow pathway hardly wide enough for his car to move forward. Yet with the tall grasses of corn brushing by the side of both the glass frames of his car, he rode through them till he reached the hut. The hut was somewhat primitive in appearance, the top thatched with palm leaves, the flooring rough surfaced with granite rocks shaped to fit hard flooring and fitted on the floor without cementing them. But the granite rocks were

well sharpened to make smooth flooring. There was only one wide room inside the hut which served the purpose for a kitchen, bedroom and front area. All these they could see as the door to the hut was opened even though there was nobody present there. They looked around for the inmates but they were nowhere around. So they had no other option but to wait there till they turned up.

After what seemed rather a long time, from the distant fields, they could see three figures approaching towards them from afar. One hour passed and the figures were clearly visible. A tall person dressed in plain working clothes, followed by a woman who was similarly dressed in plain clothes advanced towards them. A boy ran beside them, almost trotting to keep up with them.

Bhasker's Mum was intently studying the boy running by their side. She saw that he was rather tall for his age as Bhasker had informed her earlier that he was ten years old. So now he must be fifteen years.

When they reached the place, the man came forward and said," Hello! My name is Pearson. Why are you all here in this lonely place? This is my wife and her name is Alice. This is our son and his name is Prem."

When Mum, Bhasker and Anna heard this, they were surprised to hear the boy's name. They looked at one another as this was a strange coincidence.

Bhasker looked at Pearson and said, "We have met before in Delhi and I hope you do remember. If you can recollect the time you had your son admitted on a rare symptom that you could not find out. I was there in that hospital"
Pearson immediately realized that he was facing the most

187

renowned physician who was available in Delhi. So he prostrated before Bhasker, much to the surprise of the others.

"My dear Sir, What brings you to this remote area? I have nothing to offer for a great Doctor like you." he pleaded.

"You can help me by answering my questions truthfully as you know it. We have come from afar for the purpose of knowing more about your son," said Bhasker.

"Do you mean my son Prem?" he said shockingly.

"Yes! That's it. I already know a lot about him, his delirious excitement at times about a plane crash that he seemed to remember in which there was his mother, and how he remembered saving other people's lives. He even mentioned he remembered the horrifying incident so vividly."

"But that was all taken to be mad ravings of a child struck with high fever. He were discharged from the hospital after the fever had subsided," Pearson added.
"True, that was the report but there are more mysteries in our life that we can't unravel."

The son who was listening to the conversation with his mother was not at all moved by the course of events discussed in the conversation. They were looking curiously at the strangers who had come to see them. When questioned by the father, the boy had forgotten all the past episodes enacted at the hospital some years back. He had now grown bigger as five years have passed since that time. By now the boy could not remember anything what had transpired when he had been delirious on bed in the past.

Sensing that his Mum was disappointed that the search had not proved anything beyond mere heresy, Bhasker asked Pearson to relate the incidents of what had happened at the hospital.

Pearson started by saying, "Five years before, something strange was noted in the behavior of my child, Prem here. He always woke up shouting that there was a plane crash and that he was there in the plane with his mother. Several times this was repeated that he was rushed to the super specialty hospital where I had met you. You gave me peace of mind by saying that there was nothing to worry about it. It did pass off after the fever had diminished. After doses of the medicines given to him, he recovered completely from the strange hallucination that was tormenting his brain for some time. Now he is perfectly all right and never mentions such hallucinations."

"How comes that he is called Prem as that name don't seem to fit your family," Bhasker said.

"Five years back he wanted that name. It was my son who suggested so, "he said.

"Oh! I see that you're now really talking on the subject. From your talk, I understand that the events related by your son years back holds true on the subject of reincarnation. I see that he remembers the early stages of his childhood, his previous birth or slight emotional events related to his past life. Doctors haven't even yet diagnosed the cause of his mind's instability at that time."

Bhasker then pointed at his mother standing by his side, "My mother here is the subject of our talk .Her younger son, Prem was killed in the plane crash fifteen years ago. She was in that plane but she managed to escape. She hadn't recovered from the tragic shock yet."

Pearson was shocked to hear a distinguished doctor say these words. So he said," Do you really believe in reincarnation about life?"

"Circumstances and your son's mutterings years back were enough to cement the truth."

Bhasker saw at that moment that his mother had embraced the boy with his actual Mum looking on. Anna was also seen conversing in a low tone, presumably telling her why they were here.

"Pearson, if you desire, we could develop a healthy relationship. We don't plan to take your son away from you but give the freedom for my Mum to see your son whenever she wishes. You'd stand to gain much from it," said Bhasker.

"Much obliged to be of service to a great family if that'd please your Mum." said Pearson.
Bhasker felt relieved as he knew that his Mum would have peace of mind thinking that her son is finally back in another shape, close by her side. Bhasker felt that he ought to do something for his Mum. He realized that a holiday to Johor, Malaysia would be the best he could offer.
With this thought in his mind, he said, "Pearson, There's something you must agree with me. Will you allow us to take your son with us for a few months? He'll be as one of the family."

Pearson's face turned white for a moment as he grasped the meaning implied in the doctor's request. "Do you mean, you want to take my son from me?" he asked surprisingly.

"No, not in that sense, if you're willing, it's only for a short time. Your son can see the outside world, you know, "said Bhasker.

"Well! It's rather queer, "said Pearson.

"But where are you planning to take him?" he asked eagerly.

"Well! Wherever we go, we'll take care of him." said Bhasker. Bhasker was pleased at Pearson's submissiveness. He saw his mother talking excitedly with the boy, seemingly excited in doing so. Her mind was aroused by the fact that her son had come back to her in another guise. For Bhasker, the whole idea was absurd but the father's statements regarding the boy's outbursts in the past could not be ruled out as mere imagination. Many strange things had happened and this appeared to be one of them... None of us could have explored the unknown.

The next few weeks Bhasker had planned the journey to the land of his birth. He had longed to see the country where he had been brought up. He was taking Anne, his mother and even the boy whom his mother always wanted by her side. It was rather queer to note the attachment she had for the boy. The parents had agreed to hand their son to her care for some time.
After Bhasker had received the air tickets for all in the family, he called Anne and when she appeared, he asked, "Would you like a trip to Malaysia?"

"Of course, when are you planning it?" She asked excitedly.

"I have already made all the arrangements. Here are the air tickets for the family." he said.

"You mean your Mum is coming along too." She asked.

"Sure, dear, that's the country where my father was cremated. Besides her, I'm taking the boy with us."

"Do you think Prem will come?"

'Oh! He follows my mum everywhere now."

CHAPTER 9   EERIE MOMENTS

Eerie moments

A distant remote island, one hour boat ride through the rough sea or rather, more accurate to say, an island that was hardly two kilometers in width and one kilometer in length on the vast expanse of the sea near Penang harbour... A resort built specially for foreigners with all seven- star facilities was the only noticeable building worthy of a special importance on the island as foreigners from different countries crowded the place. This is the ideal place that attracted nature lovers to flock at this tiny destination, as it fulfilled all the desires that a person could have wished for. The strangeness of the place had been attributed to those pleasure-seekers, with an adventurous spirit or thirst to see something out of the ordinary, the love for adventure in a lonely island inherent in the minds of many, who were fascinated by the story of Robinson Crusoe, as related by Daniel Defoe. Many of the tourists were of the mind, that it would be a wonderful moment for them to be marooned on an island, to experience the thrill as they had read the story. Among the tourists, Anna, Bhasker, his Mum and Prem had arrived on the scene in the early morning flight. Being exhausted, they had fallen asleep in an expensive suite in the resort.

The island was desolate as it was viewable as a tiny spot from Penang harbour. Ships, ferries, Chinese junks in the shape of old boats sailed to and fro near to the harbour. The sight of men, women riding these large sampans on the sea were really admirable. Most of them were Malays and Chinese and they cheerfully rode these junk type boats to take the tourists to the nearby islands. There were young lady drivers who braved the hazards they faced in the sea by transporting the foreigners to these places close by; they were rewarded by cash collection much beyond their expectations. The beauty of the surrounding sea around was indeed admirable and tourists arrived on the scene to admire the natural beauty of the place. For miles around, the sea was thronged by endless number of Chinese boats sailing to Penang. The exquisite beauty of Penang harbour equals Singapore.

Penang, an important port in Malaysia was quite close to Indonesia, a large island where volcanoes were spread out. The dangers of volcanic eruptions were a usual occurrence.

A guide whom Bhasker had engaged to show them around came rushing inside the resort where they had taken lodging. Yusuf bangs persistently at the door where Bhasker is lodged.

Bhasker: (Alarmed!) What's the matter? Won't you allow me to take rest after the day's journey?

Yusuf: (saying hesitatingly) the….. The….. News!

Bhasker: What news!! Are you mad! (Opening the door hesitatingly).

Yusuf: Yes! Mad enough! You will be too….. When you hear…… the news?

Bhasker: (irritated) Spill it...... then.

Yusuf: BBC news, I...... I have heard the news repeatedly. It has nearly frozen...... my blood.

Bhasker: Tell me..... The news, quick!

Yusuf: The....... The....... (His teeth chatter ring) the Tsunami.

Bhasker: What Tsunami! What do you mean?

Yusuf: Reported...... Tsunami comes...... soon...

Bhasker: Where? You mean..... Tidal waves.

Yusuf: Yah..... Yes, Tsunami strikes within twenty-four hours. That I heard in the BBC news.

Bhasker: What!! You mean here. How can you understand? You don't even know the accent. How can it be intelligible to you then?

Yusuf: But I see the news flashed on the monitor. As I read it, I am stunned, stupefied and thinking of the situation...... unimaginable..... About to kill us all.

Bhasker: Don't...... Don't make me to panic...... I don't believe it.

Yusuf: You'll.......BBC Station broadcast..... It's true.
Bhasker: This is totally insane. It appears as a delusion. Isn't it a conjecture that could be renounced as it can be injudiciously perceived as an aberration in the true sense?

195

Yusuf: No! No! It's true...... The news.... People now know..... All are outside.

Bhasker: what will transpire now.......? We are in the midst of an Island..... Sea all round us..... My God! (Getting panicky)

Yusuf: We're about to recite the Koran...... the main verses in praise of the Lord!

Bhasker: Will it help? I hear the thunderous roar of the sea all round. Are we not in a small island? Let me go outside. The time nears midnight. My god! If it is true what he says, I..... I...don't even know what is going to happen. God dam place here .... Surrounded by the sea on all sides.... No place or way to escape. Oh my God!

Yusuf: The people are assembled outside, are running like mad from the impending doom.
Bhasker: Where can we scatter! The immensity of the approaching tidal waves can swallow up the island to its depths. All are fated to die by suffocating, drowning...... a horrible end......

Bhasker sees that the streets are not deserted. The tourists are standing outside staring at the sea, all pitch black, far out to the sea...
Stepping back into the resort, he sees that the majority of the tourists have realized the danger coming up from the sea.

"My goodness!!" he exclaims, 'The tourists are alarmed. How astonishingly the news spread! All realizing...... the end of the world nears...... almost all are up from their slumber, realizing escape from the oncoming gigantic waves is impossible....... Waves that can easily devour the entire

196

island……..within a second….. The island hardly measures 1.5 km in width and 1 km in length.

Thomas, the General Manager of the resort steps towards Bhasker and says, "Hello! Bhasker! Have you heard the news?"

Bhasker: Yes. What will happen…..?

Thomas: No need to panic! This has occurred before… Our resort is supposed to be the safest place around…… from the onslaught of Tsunami….. If at all it arises!

Bhasker: Is it possible it may not strike?

Thomas: Most probably, .yes. BBC has given the alert signal……. Like a hissing dragon of ancient tales, it may spring on us……causing havoc and destruction to some of the islands that may be lost forever.

Bhasker: What if it happens?

Thomas: Let's us pray and hope it doesn't. We are closed on all sides by the immeasurable vastness of the sea. There are no ways to escape from this accursed place.

Moreover the reported news by BBC, based on scientific data, can't be waived aside.

Bhasker: "My Lord! It's horrible to think of my wife and mother here for a holiday tour. Moreover that innocent boy is here.

Thomas: We can't do anything about it. But, Let us hope it will not be as disastrous as it is reported. BBC warns everyone to be alert to take precautions in case of an eventuality. But…… the island is closed on all sides by the sea……. And this is quite close to Indonesia…

Anna (comes running)   Bhasker! I'm really in a fix. This may be the only place we can be together....... Is it really true? I must know the truth. I just heard the news. Has this tsunami struck here before?

Bhasker: No! I don't think so. No one has mentioned it before. This tsunami has erupted from the effects of the thunderous explosion of a volcano in Indonesia. Such quakes happen once in a while. The pressure from below the deep sea gives rise to a tremendous surge within. That is how gigantic tidal waves are formed.

Thomas: (stepping forward) I really appreciate your knowledge. The tourists are excited and frightened..... Dammed afraid.... I should say..... It is the end of the world for us all.

Bhasker: You... you mean there's no hope for anyone.

Thomas: Not at all if it happens..... No way of escape as such an uprising could end us all in a horrible death by drowning. But let us all hope it does not strike.

Bhasker: how can that be! Can they give false reports?

Thomas: No! I didn't mean that. Sometimes miracles can happen.
Bhasker: Natural calamities can happen at any moment anywhere. We have to face them.

An announcement is heard from loudspeakers in the resort.

"Gigantic waves rising at a height of three stories have

devastated and swept away everything in the coastal areas in Japan... Thousands of people are killed, drowned and swept away by the killer waves. Homes of hundreds are lost and destroyed as destruction has laid waste on these areas. The killer waves are moving forward as a missile with a target for destruction on the islands near to Indonesia and Sumatra."

The tourists had heard the announcement and ran madly outside but they were stopped in their tracks when they heard another announcement that help was on the way. Bhasker went inside and brought his Mum, Anna and the boy outside to be ready in case of an eventuality.

 The sounds of helicopters were heard in the far distance. Small specks in the distant sky became larger and larger as they approached near. Yusuf hurried and engaged in announcing to all to gather outside for the way of escape. Within minutes the thundering ear-splitting sounds of the helicopters were audible to everyone. The helicopters numbering twelve came down in the wide strip of open space available in front of the resort. All the tourists including the local people, few in numbers got into the copters. When all had embarked, a search was made to find if anyone one was left behind. Then the signal was given for take-off and the copters took off to the skies amidst a deafening roaring sound emitted from the engines.

But Bhasker noticed something queer happening as he chanced to look outside. The waves encircling the island were seen to be rising rapidly as they neared the shore. Bhasker was seated near the side .So he could see clearly the sights as the copter circled the island. As they watched, the sea had risen to a gigantic height, and swallowed the small stretch of island smashing down the trees, uprooting them within a split second. All were shocked to see the whole island sub-merged under the sea.

Anna, who saw the disastrous, natural calamity down below could only say," My God! What'd have happened if we were down there?"

Bhasker's Mum merely muttered," Everything happens when it has to happen?"

Bhasker took last moment photo flashes of the scenes down in the island.

The beauteous ocean had always excited Bhasker. Watching the wondrous splashing of the foamy waves as it lashed against the rocks at the shore and more wondrous still; the spin, as the waves rose and crashed down-wards in a tumultuous roar had excited him in his younger days to a state of tranquility and peace.

He had often marveled at the beauty of nature especially the vast blue sea. But its hideous disastrous nature as a rogue made him realize there was a different picture to it. A sea adventure was what he had always hoped for in his inquisitiveness to learn more.

He remembered setting out with his friend at an early age. He was then in the prime of youth and ready to face any danger. He was twenty-five years old at that time. Early in the morning, he had gone to the deep sea. The incessant swaying of the boat swirling forward unsteadily in the deep sea by the force of the mighty waves had caused an uneasiness in his stomach, forcing him to vomit intermittently. But his friend had no such uneasiness as he was accustomed to sea voyages.

After some time he had recovered and was immediately taken back by the sight of some dolphins following the boat in rapid swishing strokes. The sea was so pleasant and the dolphins seemed so playful and enchanting to behold that he was not able to resist an irresistible desire to be amongst their midst to enjoy the fun. He jumped into the sea dimly unaware of the hidden dangers that lurked under the depths.

Almost immediately, a large shark revealing razor sharp teeth opened its jaws wide and lunged for him. He was so shocked that he desperately looked about him. As the jaws of death was about to snap at him, he felt helpless and realized that his end was near. In his fright, he closed his eyes. After a few seconds, when he opened his eyes, he saw that the shark had disappeared and dolphins were playing about by his side.

He realized that that the dolphins had been his savior and he started following them in easy powerful strokes. But his friend had warned him not to go to the depth for long. The desire to be along with the dolphins for some moment kept him enjoying their company. Almost immediately another shark came to the surface in front of him He felt trapped as in a nightmare incident. The shark opened its jaws exposing powerful teeth that could slice him to pieces.
Before the jaws could snap shut on him, two dolphins blocked him by surfacing in front of him. In the hassle and tussle that took place, the monster was driven from him by the powerful thrust of the snouts. Feeling secure in their company, he played for some more time, while his friend was

apprehensive of dangers that may arise at any moment. But really he had nothing to fear as long as the dolphins were by his side.

Back in Johor, their home

There were dangers, no doubt, beneath the depths. He had not that eerie feeling that surmounted him at this moment as he had experienced in the past. He had the company of the dolphins to shield him from the cruel jaws of death. Now it was different. His Anna, mum, and the boy were with him and he was concerned more for their safety. Anna had not spoken in the copter. His mum was seated close to the boy, embracing and reassuring him.

When the copters landed at Penang away from the harbour, they lost sight of the sea. They were taken to an expensive hotel. Bhasker had decided that the next trip would be to Johor, the place where his Mum had brought him up as a child. He decided to hire a taxi that would travel fast along the roadway. His Mum and Anna were excited when they learned about it.

Early in the morning they started. The time was still before dawn as the roads were still lighted from the glow of the street lamps. As the car sped on, a cold breeze blew on the faces of Prem who was dozing by the side. Mother was cuddling him as though she was afraid that she would lose him again. Anna had fallen asleep by the side of Mum. Bhasker was in the front by the side of the driver. Slowly in the distance he saw the bright brilliant redness of the sky as the sun started its ascent upwards in the heavens. The sky appeared to be blanketed with a glowing red as if the heavens had unfolded its brightness to lighten up the world from the darkness. Slowly and steadily the sun was seen moving up straight ahead to dazzle the world with life giving rays.

Bhasker admiring the beauty exclaimed, "What a beauty! Heaven unfolds the glory of the world for all to admire."

Anna close behind to him was also enthralled by the beauty revealed to her sight. She said, 'truly a fascinating sight to behold!' she remarked.

Mum was also looking at the sky. "She said after looking at Prem, " I admire the greatness of heaven's glory when I think of Prem but now as he's here, I have nothing to admire in it,"

As the car entered the countryside road, the fields of corn swaying continuously in the gentle breeze had an effect on Anna's mind. She felt like a country woman in her imagination. Her mind traveled far away and she saw herself as a country woman quite thrilled to reap the ripe corns and grains that stretched endlessly on the vast plains. She had never seen countryside with harvests ripe for the picking.

After hours of driving through the open ground, the road entered a forest area. The road started winding up and down, sometimes turning in a zigzag direction a narrow path that was filled with dust as vehicles passed the way. On both sides of the road, giant trees with thick foliage were huddled close together. It was nearing dusk and Bhasker knew that they were almost near to their destination. Rubber trees also were spread out like a forest on both sides. It was getting dark as the sun had set. The setting sun was hidden by the mass foliage of rubber trees that stretched endlessly in a never ending line.

He looked back at his mother to see her reaction on seeing the place. It was here that he and Prem had spent their childhood... Their father had worked as a police officer. He could see clearly his father and visualize him coming towards them with a rifle in his hand. He could recollect the day, his father had taken him to see the man-eater that he had shot. The man-eater had been a terror for the Tamil- workers in the rubber plantation killing several lady workers and children. When Bhasker had seen the man-eater, he was terror-struck. Bhasker was hardly thirteen years of age. The man-eater was a ferocious tiger of massive size, and Bhasker had heard its roaring sound more than once, which was enough to freeze or chill the blood of any humans, who crossed its path. So when he saw the enormous carcass of the tiger, he wondered that his father was more than a human to have killed it. He wondered then how his younger brother would have reacted if he had been there with him. But he knew that his brother was different from him. On losing his brother at the air-crash, he knew he had lost him forever. Now how could that boy who, ignorant of his past at present, could be a substitute of the real one.

As they reached the place that was to be their home for the holidays, Bhasker's Mum nudged Anna and said excitedly, "That was our home when my husband was alive. Both my sons had grown up here.

"And it looks the same. No changes have taken place." she continued. Bhasker had heard of many eerie incidents from his mother of his dad's exploits. The most tragic incident had been narrated by his mother years back. He used to hear it from her occasionally.

• About the distant past, in those days, his mother used to say many real incidents of the past about her husband. The story goes on and on----

• Bhasker's father gropes his way onward in the night, feeling his boots sinking in the muddy path. A heavy downpour made the path so clayey that walking along the forest area was a tedious task even for a person hardly accustomed to the jungle area. The rain poured on endlessly for some time but when it subsided into a mere drizzling, his Papa trudges on along the path to his home at the edge of the forest.

The place around was in total darkness and it was a time when predators roamed the wild in search of prey. Human habitations were non-existent for miles around as Papa steps further onwards into the forest area. The place where he had stayed was amidst a clearing, a house built specially for a Supervisor and family. There was a long clearing through the area that had served as a pathway to enter the house.

.By his side trod the only companion that he knew was so dear to him. When he was with him, Papa felt no fear of any lurking danger, which may perchance come forward in his way. Both of them felt a close relationship not shared before by anybody whom Papa had known. At times his friend's mere size and ferocious look kept strangers away at a distance. Papa's friend never seemed to disengage himself from him even for a second. He accompanied him to the bar where he had overstayed till late at night, owing to the heavy rain. When the rain was over, his friend nudged him as if to signal that it had been already late. Papa realized that he had been cared for as his friend was so concerned for his master's safety.

His anxiety for Papa was not without a cause for the area

205

around was not safe to wander aimlessly at night. Dangerous carnivores always prowled the area seeking prey. Papa had stepped on the road, the darkness outside blinding him. Having forgotten to carry a torch that seemed a handy weapon, he had felt inclined to rely on the assistance of his friend to lead him on. His friend led the way, and Papa followed closely behind. For some time there was no sort of communication between them even by gesture. He was hardly noticeable in the hideous darkness that enveloped them as they moved on. Papa could only follow at his heels by quickening his pace and he had found it extremely difficult to keep up with him. They had followed a road that led to a thick jungle.

They had neared the open ground where the gruesome jungle started and had seen his house from a distance in the darkness. Papa had felt a premonition of some danger he could not understand. Almost immediately there was a deep growling sound from his friend but he had seen nothing that had caused his friend to react in this way. Papa had no torch that he could use to find out the cause of the disturbance arising in his friend.

His friend was an immensely huge bull of a dog and he was extremely fond of Papa and would go to any length to protect him. The Administrator had gifted the dog to him three years ago. Now they had become so fond of each other and they felt they could not be separated even for a moment. The incessant growling in spite of his   protests brought a sense of alarm. Looking over his shoulder, four pairs of eyes glittered in the pitch darkness catching Papa's attention.

Frantically Papa searched in his pocket for the pistol he had always carried with him. He somehow realized that he had left it in the house. Imagine the shock, Papa felt when he saw a ferocious, deadly tiger near to them, watching and waiting. Papa realized the pitiable and helpless situation they were facing now, for if the tiger charged, they would have no chance. Papa immediately sensed that he had to move slowly backwards. He knew a tiger was damn fast in its movements.

Then Papa saw in the dim light the gate. He opened the gate and glided into the house. Almost at that split second, the tiger with a ferocious roar, charged. But the bull dog intercepted by falling straight at the carnivore. The bull dog was ripped apart by a mighty blow that smashed its skull. But in that instant second, Papa had got in and locked the gate. His dog, though it was huge in size was not a match for the tiger. Papa had buried his dearest friend's remains inside the compound of this house.

This vivid account of the tragedy that had occurred years ago was still imprinted in Mom's memory and had been told to Bhasker several times.

When they reached their destination, the house there appeared to have an uncanny appearance. Most of the parts of the house were dilapidated and some bamboos that made the doors and windows were missing, while others broken. The place around had a desolate look as it had not been occupied for years. The gloominess of the place was intensified by the thick jungle, surrounded by tall dense trees that rose high up to the sky, shielding away the brightness of the sun. The place around was enclosed in semi-darkness throughout the day. The natural beauty of the area was admirable but not without hidden dangers. In such dense foliage of trees and tall bushes that had not been cut for years, wild animals roaming the place is a possibility.

For miles there was not a sign of human habitations as this was the only house built in the past for the Supervisor to inspect the rubber plantations and the forest. This had been his father's home where they had stayed for many years in the distant past.

Now the place was said to be a haunted house. The local people who lived further down amidst the rubber plantations never dared to approach the area. They said that an old lady and her husband had lived there for some years. The husband had been the senior supervisor who was skilled in the use of firearms. But their mysterious death had baffled all the local people. Most of the workers in the area were Tamilians while there were Chinese and Malays among them. But all had been shocked to see the mutilated bodies of the supervisor and his wife. The man's right arm had been plucked off the shoulders and the skull smashed. The woman's skull had been smashed and her hair wrenched off her skull. Further there had been no sign to indicate that it was a wild animal, as none of the parts had been bitten and eaten.

The mystery regarding their death had been unresolved till Bhasker, his mum, Anna and Prem came on the scene. The people believed that evil spirits may be behind the murder. So they advised Bhasker to drop the idea of staying there. But Bhasker was not superstitious enough to believe the false presumptions of the people. Anna and his Mum agreed with him. Prem, the boy who accompanied them was silent. He was matured enough to express his feelings as he was eighteen years of age. But, he believed that he was not yet of their family even though the old lady, Bhasker's Mum had said so .She had told him that he had raved forth the past about them but he didn't remember having said it.

His father had also reminded him of that, but he considered all these false assumptions, as vague recollections that had no proof.

It was a haunted house all right according to the local community. The people of that area were aware of sinister frightful sounds inside that house at midnight. No one dared to inspect what was really happening in that weird house. The house was of immense size with lots of rooms specially built for the convenience of a family who were residing at Malaysia. The Company had built that house as they wanted the Supervisor's family to live there comfortably. But a terrible accident had happened and a husband and wife were killed mysteriously at the spot. It has been supposed that the departed souls of this family were hovering aimlessly in this house. Much has been said by the people around that the house has been haunted in the stillness of midnight for a long time. No one dared to occupy or buy that house for fear something dreadful may happen to them. The house had not been repainted or cleaned for years. It remained abandoned in that condition. Nobody intervened or enquired of the family who had expired so tragically. None of the relatives wanted to have anything to do with the affairs of the house. They feared that something dreadful may happen to anyone of them if they tried to live in the house. But some of the people came forward to live there for a night. But they could not outlast even an hour at midnight inside as the fearful apparitions were seen, that made them flee for their lives. Bhasker knew that the people were foolish to have these false notions of evil spirits haunting the place. He had no fear of ghosts or the spirits which moved in the darkness. He used to scoff at the very idea of people panicking in fear of ghosts which according to him, do not exist but the wayward hallucinations revolving in the minds of people seized emotionally with fear of the Unknown. Many had deliberately made an attempt to stay overnight at that place to see for themselves the truth about the ghostly talks by the people. When they had entered the house at night, everything was quite peaceful around the place but the house was in an untidy condition as it had not been used for years. Moreover they had noticed that most of the furniture was thrown about as if the place had been ransacked recently. They hadn't known how long they had overslept, but they reported that they were awakened by something pulling at their throats... They had found nothing there. The tightening around their throat had disappeared. Then they had seen a figure of a girl with hair loosened, eyeing them from a distance. They had a sudden shock and fright when they realized that they were fully awake. They had tried to shout at the ghostly figure but it disappeared as it had come. Then they reported that they had noticed more phantom figures hurrying about the place which had a hallowing appearance about them. Now they had realized that the people were right in their assumptions that the place was truly haunted by spirits. It was truly natural for them to believe about ghosts. There is nothing surprising for them to suppose that supernatural events related by others were after all true as they were led to believe the truth of the supernatural after seeing it themselves. So they had left the place immediately as they did not want to interfere with unworldly beings which seemed to wander about the place.

It was towards this very place that Bhasker had taken accommodation along with his Mum, Anna and Prem. Mum didn't feel anything queer about the place it had been her home years back. She was unaware of the recent developments and the horror narrated by the occupants in the nearby area.

Night had fallen when they reached the house. In the darkness the taxi driver had lost the way more than once. But finally they had reached the place. There was a man in front of the house who had been waiting for their arrival. He was an old man whose face was sunken and his eyes had the piercing look that would freeze one's blood.

He was shabbily dressed and when he saw them, ambled towards Bhasker and said" Welcome! Rather a surprise for me as I rarely gets visitors." He handed the key to Bhasker and said, "Everything has been swept and cleaned in the morning. The place was a total mess. Now all is neat and the bedrooms and the rooms are arranged properly."

Who sent you here?" asked Bhasker.

"Why, Of course, it is the Company you have phoned for arrangements."

'But, 'said Bhasker, "The local people here told me no one comes here nowadays."

"So you know, but the mystery lies still unsolved. OK folks, have a nice time."
He left in a hurry as if he was trying to escape from a hideous danger that sill lurked about the surroundings. There were two bedrooms that were well furnished. The windows and doors of these rooms could be fastened to be secure from any interference from outside. As this was situated at the edge of the jungle, wild beasts were likely to be seen prowling around at midnight. Anna was unaware of the gossips

around, and she seemed to enjoy the sights and loneliness of the jungle she had the experience of seeing for the first time.

Bhasker's Mum had experienced the wonderful moments in her life with her husband here. Though her husband had gone forever, she had the feeling that he was with her in this room. Her adopted son, Prem had fallen asleep on the couch beside the bed. But she was wide awake and her thoughts flashed to the past when her husband was with her at this very spot. The lights in the room were dim. They needed replacement as they were old lamps. On close scrutiny, the lighting system had not been replaced for a long time .The house would have lost its eerie look if there were more lamps in the house. There were large glass window panes where Mum was sleeping. But the glass frames were strong enough to resist the breaking in of any creatures or person in the night. Since the place was without any human habitations for miles around, the place gave a creepy feeling of goose-bumps.

At around midnight, the spirits of darkness were usually out, according to the local people. The silence of the night was shattered by a piercing scream that Bhasker and Anna got up from their bed with a jerk. To his horror, he realized that it was his Mum. Bhasker ran to the other bedroom followed by Anna. Prem was up and was looking out of the window. But he didn't open it for fear. Bhasker got inside the room.
 "What is the matter? Have you had a nightmare?" he asked his mother.

"No! There was a monstrous being outside looking at me. I don't know how long it was there but the eyes were fixed on Me." she shouted.

"Did you see it clearly?" he enquired.

"Not so clearly. It had long hairy arms and hands but its legs were dangling side by side. The face appeared as though it resembled a gorilla, considering its huge size. When I screamed it vanished suddenly."

Prem said that he hadn't seen anything. He was awakened by the scream but it had disappeared when he had looked for it. Bhasker told his mother to fasten the shutters of the windows and lock the doors before turning in for the night. Meanwhile he got his revolver and oiled it. He also made sure to load it in case of emergency.

The next day a group of workers from the nearby rubber plantation came hurriedly.
One of them on seeing Bhasker said," Sahib, while we were tapping rubber, a gigantic ape- like creature appeared that looked so hideous with an arm span of several feet. The hands and legs were treble the size of our arms. It jumped at us, injuring several of us and ran away as we shouted for help."

"Where is it now?" asked Bhasker.

"Close by among the trees," said the man.
The workers looked frightened and helpless. Taking the loaded revolver, Bhasker gave the sign to guide him to the spot. Bhasker was surprised when his Mum and the others said they wanted to come along. Since there were workers with them, he did not object.

As they walked through the woods, Anna exclaimed, "What a lonely place to walk about!"

Bhasker's Mum, Smitha knew the place well though the

213

jungle had grown so thick and crowded with rubber trees so close to each other. Suddenly after having walked a long distance, one from among the group of workers shouted pointing at a high tree close to them.
"There he is".

All looked up and were shocked at the sight that they be held. A massive creature stared at them with a menacing look. Its head was similar to that of an ape and a gorilla, its hands and arms so wide and long, covered fully with matted hair. The legs of the creature appeared to be hanging closely like a chimpanzee that used both the arms and legs for swinging from trees to trees with equal ease.
Bhasker had his pistol ready in case the creature attacked. But, at that moment, something happened almost simultaneously.

Smitha who was standing a bit aside from the others uttered a frightful cry as an enormous python dropped by her side and started encircling her body. The others were caught unawares. Bhasker was desperate and Anna and Prem started screaming. Bhasker could not shoot for fear of hitting his Mum. The workers were stunned and too frightened to act. Bhasker suddenly lunged forward to disengage the huge snake before it suffocated his mother.

Almost without anyone realizing what had happened, the enormous snake was wrenched off Smitha's body to be thrown aside in a swift movement. All were amazed to watch the ape like creature caressing Smitha gently with his great paws. Smitha could not believe that a great creature like this ape had a gentle heart. She stared at the creature in disbelief. Then when she scrutinized the giant closely, she knew…..

Her husband had brought her a small monkey-like baby

when Bhasker had been very young. Her husband had found it by the side of the creature's dead mother in the forest when he was on a hunting trip. It was an orangutan or so the Malays called it, meaning man-ape. A fully grown orangutan was powerful as a gorilla. Smitha had fed it with milk and took care of it lovingly. Wherever she went she cuddled it and took it with her. When it had grown up slightly, her husband died, and she had to return back to India with her children. She had left her orangutan to the next Supervisor and his wife who had come to that place years ago.

She realized that this giant was indeed none other than her pet whom she had left behind many, many years ago. She got excited and looked closely at the orangutan as he caressed her and made slow mutterings to show that he had recognized his long lost mistress. All those present were astonished to witness this strange scene. Bhasker knew the truth now as vague recollections of a tiny orangutan running by the side of his mother eighteen years before came to his mind. He knew it then.

Anna and Prem were flabbergasted at this sight and they were puzzled. The orangutan would not budge an inch from Smitha as he showed his pleasure by gently rubbing her. Seeing an enormous giant orangutan behaving in a queer way, the simple workers thought that Smitha was a goddess. The giant monkey- like creature had been a terror to these people for a long time. Bhasker had a faint doubt regarding the cruel killing of the old man and woman found dead in the old house. They may have been killed by this gentle creature when it had turned violent, having been provoked to these heinous acts by the cruelties inflicted on it by humans. Bhasker told the men gathered there to leave for their homes.

"Don't you worry about the orangutan? My mother has tamed him."

He smiled at his Mum as he said so. Anna was perplexed and

looked at him.

When the workers gathered there who had gathered there left, he turned to Anna and said, "It's a long story and if you ask my Mum, she will tell you all about it."

When they turned to go back home, the orangutan followed Smitha as though he would never part from her. As Bhasker watched, he wondered how a ferocious wild creature could turn meek as a lamb the next moment. Then he knew that the creature still remembered the affection of his Mum years back. An animal never forgets.

Just as they reached the house at the edge of the forest, they heard loud shouts of a crowd of workers with their wives and children rushing towards them. They were carrying basket loads of fruits, bananas and other items. Bhasker could not believe what he saw. When they reached close to Smitha, they stopped in their tracks. The orangutan turned and faced them. It started emitting deep growling sounds. Bhasker warned them not to approach near as his Mum would not be able to control the orangutan.

One of the men shouted, "Sahib! We bring all these for the goddess who has tamed the violent ape that had terrorized us for a long time; we bring our wives and children to get her divine blessing,"

He said pointing at Smitha, by whose side towered the dreaded creature of the forest.

Smitha who understood what they meant, told them in Tamil to go back. She told them to return after a week and she'd receive each of them to bless them all. They understood and bowed down reverently laying down their burden. Then they departed as they had come.

Smitha felt a bit uneasy at the thought that she was revered as a goddess. She had a clear conviction that they would be back within a week in a multitude. The news that a goddess had arrived among them was likely to be inflamed as a forest fire engulfed the whole area for miles. The people would flock to her as they believed she had descended from a divine existence to help them.

The gentle orangutan who walked lovingly by her side had been deprived off the love and affection at an early age. He had never known what it was to be loved other than the moments he had with Smitha. Naturally that remembrance was stamped in his memory. An animal never forgets and that was what reawakened that sense of longing to be loved by someone. He had presumably been cruelly treated by all the people and that could have been the reason he had become so savage. He had escaped into the jungle and in course of time had turned against the people who might have cruelly treated him. Smitha was determined to keep her pet reunited with her and the boy Prem. No matter where she went, she would take them with her. The orangutan, she believed was her priced possession given to her by her husband, years back. She would not lose him again. But she knew she could not keep him for long as she had to return to her country. As the thoughts of leaving the orangutan were troubling her mind, she heard uproar outside.

Smitha saw Bhasker, Anna talking with a crowd of the local people gathered there. They had brought their family with them. Smitha knew why they had come but she didn't expect them this soon. She wanted to be with them but the orangutan was by her side. She saw him glaring at the crowd as if his intention was to wreck havoc on them. Smitha tried to appease the ferocious giant by gently caressing him.

Then she approached the crowd with the orangutan following by her side. Prem watched from a distance as he

217

wondered why the people had come there. As the crowd saw the dreaded creature advancing towards them with the goddess who they believed Smitha to be, they all fell on their knees. Smitha felt rather foolish for they had brought many varieties of items which were costly to them. She knew that whatever she might say to them could not change their minds to believe that she was not a goddess.

She talked gently to the crowd in Malay, the language she had learned before. They were stupefied and listened to her. They realized she was indeed a goddess, else how could she talk their mother tongue so fluently.

Smitha said, "You all think of me as a goddess but I'm not. I'm a human being like you all. So you need not get any false notion about me."
But one from among the crowd shouted, "No! We know you are a goddess. No one else can tame a wild orangutan that had been a terror to us lately."

"Some of you may have abused him, else how could he have acted so ferociously?"

Smitha mingled with them for some time but warned them not to come near her, for fear of rousing the orangutan that stayed near, waiting and watching. After a while they left the place when they got an assurance from Smitha that she would be amongst them for some time in future.

After they had left, Bhasker said," Mum! I have just received a call from the Health Department in India. I'm told to report immediately back as they have an urgent message for me"
"What's the message, my son," she asked.
"They didn't tell, mum," he said.

Hearing the talk, Anna enquired, "When do we return?"

"Immediately- I have got the return tickets confirmed for all of us" he said.

"What?" asked Smitha, "But do you think I'd leave without my pet."

"Which pet, you mean," asked Bhasker.

"I mean the orangutan." she said.

"But…. How can we take the animal that belongs here," Bhasker asked.

"Then I can't go back without him." she said.

"Mum! Don't be so foolish! We can't do it. He belongs here", Bhasker said.

"No! He doesn't. He belongs to me." mum said

Bhasker knew he could not argue with his mother once she had made up her mind. She was adamant and he knew it. So he merely said, "I'll see what can be done."

Anna looked at him, trying to figure out what he had in his mind.

An intruder in the forest.

Violent shouts and cries from a group of people were heard nearby. They ran almost madly towards our home. One of them shouted hysterically, "Save us! Oh! Goddess! A fierce looking creature was seen in the forest. It came down at us during the night."

"We're afraid to go out in the forest where we have to

work." said another man.

"We'll try to find the creature" said Bhasker.

He had his revolver with him.

But Smitha came forward and said, "No, Bhasker, don't go with them now. It is nearly dusk and night fast approaching. Tell them to come tomorrow," she said.

When they were gone, the surrounding area was engulfed in semi-darkness. Partial brightness from the luminous moon spread to lighten up the place.

"Who could have been the mysterious creature?" asked Anna when Bhasker was beside her.

"They didn't mention it," he said, "Maybe we'll know tomorrow."

When they retired for the night, mother left the orangutan to lie outside.

The night was peaceful and all slept soundly.

Next day at daybreak, Bhasker woke up and looked outside. He was surprised to find the orangutan missing. He searched all over the place but couldn't find him. He shouted for his mother. "Mum! Wake up! Our pet is missing."

His mother came running outside with Prem. Anna was also there. Mum was shocked at her son's outburst.

"What happened? Where is my pet?" she cried.

"I...I don't know", he said.

"Where could he have disappeared?" she said.

They searched everywhere but he was nowhere to be seen.

Mother could hardly control the tears that streamed down her face.

Bhasker tried to console her. "Mum! Don't get excited! Something queer has happened."

"What do you mean?" she asked.
"He might have wandered off to the jungle on his own. He'll return." he said.

"But", she said, "We have to return within a week. Isn't that what you said." she said.

"True," he said, "I'm going in search now. I've called the local people for help."

As they waited at the entrance to the forest, a gang of men experienced in tracking the jungle appeared. They were all well built, swarthy men accustomed to the rough terrain of the jungle path.

"Let me come along," said Bhasker's mother, "I feel these men aren't enough to tackle her pet"

Anna persuaded her to stay back as the jungle was not safe. But Smitha didn't yield to Anna's persuasions.
Seeing the futility in dissuading her further, Bhasker said, "Mother, if you think you can trek through the jungle, you may come."
When they started, Prem ran to Smitha's side and begged her to take him too. Anna remained at home watching them set out through the thick overgrown jungle.

There was hardly a path for them to walk as tall bushes thickly overgrown lay stretched everywhere. Massive trees with overhanging branches were seen crowded that the sun's rays never penetrated through this thick dense jungle. The men were highly experienced in tracking wild animals in the forest. They knew the hidden dangers that lurked there. As they cautiously moved forward, they heard many strange sounds. The sounds seemed faint as if wild beasts were groaning and growling a short distance away.

Then they saw an eye-catching scene of two orangutans embracing each other. The creatures were on top of an overhanging thick branch.

One of the men said, "It is a male and a female. Let's not make a noise. That could transform them to violent, ferocious creatures."

Smitha immediately noticed her pet with another orangutan that was smaller in size. She tried to call out but Bhasker said, "No, mother. Don't disturb them."

Suddenly the orangutans saw them. They started growling menacingly but then stopped. One of them had noticed Smitha. Smitha daringly advanced towards them while the men and Bhasker waited. Both the creatures remained silent as Smitha lovingly touched them. Bhasker was surprised at his mother's daringness. The orangutans have their own way in communicating as one of them had recognized her as a mistress. Her pet seemed to be much larger in appearance than the other and it was uttering low sounds. He appeared to be telling Smitha that he had found a mate. He jumped up and down and in his frenzy, encouraged Smitha to come closer to his mate. She understood and moved closer to the female orangutan. She caressed her slowly. The female orangutan was a lovely creature with long hairy arms and legs. Her body was not so masculine like her pet. She appreciated Smitha's gentle touch; the touch with a magical power for those whom she really cared. Bhasker knew it, of course, far better than the others.

After some time, Smitha encouraged her pet to bring his mate home. But before she could make him realize what she meant, they had swung to the treetop of a huge tree and disappeared from her sight. For more than thirty minutes she

waited there with the others hoping they would return.
Bhasker said," Mother, I don't think he would return. He's
happy now as he has a mate. Both of them belong here.
Leave them in peace."

Though she was disheartened, his mother understood what
he meant. Finally they returned home.

REVIEWSFOR A PREVIOUS VERSION OF THIS BOOK
BY B.K.WALKER

My rating: 3 of 5 stars

Life Blossoms like a Rose in Thorns by Raghavan
Jayaprakash was an intriguing story.

Starting with the life of Smitha, a young Indian girl who
believes that arranged marriages should no longer be as
they were accustomed to. When her sister is arranged to
be married, Smitha is angered by the fact that the husband
is only out for her father's fortune.

Smitha is determined to break free from tradition, earning
her education hoping to be the one woman who fights for
all in India. When she learns of her brother in law's abuse
toward her sister and their children, she refuses to be put
in the same situation.

She earns her education, traveling to Ethiopia to teach. It is
here that she stumbles upon a conversation for
assassination of the president. Sure that no one will
believe her, she takes her information to the guards, as
she is even more sure that she cannot live with such
knowledge should something happen that she could have
prevented.

When she is taken seriously, and the President is saved,
she is given instant leadership by the president, where she
learns military skills and gains riches. Upon her return to

home, she is presented with multiple marriage proposals.

Much to her surprise, one man she actually felt a connection with and they were married. To her surprise, he too had wealth, and was not only after hers.

They bore two children, who were told would be great in the world. Though both children were like night and day, they both grew to make their parents proud.

After the death of her husband from a tragic accident, Smitha mourns for over a year. It is when her brother summons them home that they return to their native land.

The boys, Bhaskar and Prem, both attend private school and excel at a rapid pace. Bhaskar falls in love, only to win a scholarship where he must leave his one true love Anna behind.

After years of being gone and becoming a world class heart surgeon, he is paid a visit from his mother and brother, who left training for the Olympics to see his brother. When they land there is a tragic accident that claims his brother's life. Heartbroken and grieving, Bhaskar decides to call his lost love, only to learn she has married another.

The years pass, and Bhaskar is called to an emergency heart surgery to save a wealthy Indian. As he boards the plane he sees a familiar face. "Good Morning Anna, how are you my Dear?" Shocked at the appearance of one that Anna thought was lost forever, she is more than happy to see her long lost love. After the flight they get together where they talk of the past and learn neither is married. They both agree to wait no longer and marry in a private ceremony before Bhaskar is scheduled for surgery.

The surgery was a huge success, Bhaskar is deemed a hero, and the love between him and Anna only grows deeper.

This was a great story. The only thing I had a problem with was that there was no notice of change in character. This title is entirely in the first person, and switches to first person of another character with no advance notice. I loved to learn about how there is wish to change customs in India, and found Smitha a very strong and empowering woman. I think the story could have ended better, having Anna meet Smitha and seeing her reaction to an interracial marriage by her son.

I give Life Blossoms like a Rose in Thorns ***1/2 (3.5) Stars, BK Walker.

Life Blossoms like a Rose in Thorns by Raghavan Jayaprakash

Two reviews:

Review 1: This book was a very great and inspirational read. Smitha
is the main character and she is a rebel. She cannot stand

the way that the women of her Indian culture are treated.
She speaks to her mom about her opinions on the matter and
her mother just says there is nothing they can do about
it; our culture has always been this way. Smithas father
dies and her mother leans on her son in law for support.
He treats her unfairly, due to the way women were treated
as inferiors to men at the time. Smitha gets very upset
about the situation and goes out and speaks of how men
and women are equals. Smitha ends up getting married and
settles down. She has one son in the book and she is not
treated as an inferior by her husband. I really liked this
book and found it inspirational to women of every background and culture.
This book was very inspirational with the way Smitha stood up for what she believed in. This book can be inspirational to women everywhere. It relates to many women's problems. Smitha is like an average teenage girl who rebels and so teenage girls can relate to this book as well. Teenage girls can learn independence from Smitha's story. This book was a great read and very inspirational.

Reviewer Age: 15
Reviewer City, State and Country: Keiser, Arkansas America

Review 2: Thoroughly thought provoking and truthful, this is the story of a young Hindu woman named Smitha, following her through her teenage years, and then onto her adult life. She does not agree with her religion's (Hindu's) view on arranged marriages, and watching as her sister's marriage falls and crumbles, she wishes to have a choice in which she marries and so sets out on a quest to become someone in the world.
Written in four sections, each follows a different part of her life, it switches in part three to following her son Bhaskar's storey. Set in the late 1940's and onward, it is a storey that fully reminds the you, the reader, of the free life we have ; women treated with equal status and rights not just a possession of their husband. Like books such as '(un)arranged marriage' by Bali Rai, as a reader you come to understand a little more of what it would be like to have your life planned for you. As in the books mentioned above, Smitha is determined not to be shaped and molded by her parents and influential figures around her, and this is what she sets out to do. The 'voice', in which it is written, is not amusing or soft, but quite the opposite; it tells it like it is.

Personally, I found it hard to relate too, due to the fact it is written so bluntly, but it does get to the point quickly. The ending comes together well, with only one question left un-answered but then the question in its self is a little confusing! Even though the pace of the storey is rather fast, it's a light read and short too, at approx 160 pages. I would recommend this book for you if you enjoy religious books about other culture or story about women's rights and it would be a great study tool in Religious Education!

I would only recommend this book to mature readers, due to the sexual content that it contains.
Reviewer Age: 14
Reviewer City, State and Country: Swindon, Wiltshire England

ABOUT THE AUTHOR

Jayaprakash Raghavan Pillai was born in Johore. He had his secondary education in Kuala Lumpur, Malaysia. After his father expired, he returned to India. He is a Master in English Literature. He has worked as an expatriate teacher in Ethiopia, Africa and Maldives.

He has published many Articles and Poems. His three books " Life Blossoms Like a Rose in Thorns" , "Poems That Thrill", "Eerie Moments" have been published.

His writings reflect the moments that he had experienced in the countries like Malaysia, Ethiopia, Africa The author's short story "Hijacking That Failed" was published when he was an Expatriate Teacher in Ethiopia. His three other Books, "Life Blossoms Like a rose in Thorns" ; "Poems That Thrill"; "Eerie Moments" have been published in the year 2009. The background of these writings were his experiences when he was abroad.

List of other writings by Jayaprakash Raghavan Pillai on several Websites displayed.

1)His short story "The Young Princess" was published by the Latin Heritage Foundation in a collection of stories in the book " The Smartest kid in the Bronx" at Amazon.

2)His One Act Drama for 90 minutes of Hospital Drama titled " Why Affairs Happen" was published by "OFF THE WALL PLAYS".

3)His Poems were published on websites: a)voicenet.com (12poems)

b) poemhunter.com(6poems)
c)amazon.com

4)His book " The Story She Had to Tell' was published by feedaread.com

5)Jayaprakash Raghavan Pillai-Boloji.com
POEMS-18
MEMOIRS-2
RAMBLINGS-1
SHORT STORIES-2
WORKSHOP-

www.ingramcontent.com/pod-product-compliance
Lightning Source LLC
LaVergne TN
LVHW091215080426
835509LV00009B/1013